# New Treasury
## of
# Handmade Gifts

# New Treasury
# of
# Handmade Gifts

Edited by Kate Yeates

ANAYA PUBLISHERS LTD
LONDON

First published in Great Britain in 1994
by Anaya Publishers Ltd, Strode House,
44–50 Osnaburgh Street, London NW1 3ND

With thanks to Judy Taylor, Wendy Gardiner
and Audrey Vincente Dean for providing the
designs in this book.

British Library Cataloguing-in-Publication Data

A catalogue record for this book is available from
the British Library

ISBN 1 85470 234 3

Typeset by Servis Filmsetting Ltd, Manchester, UK
Printed and bound in Hong Kong

# Contents

# Introduction

*A gift you have made yourself shows that you really care and when you have this enchanting collection to choose from, it will be a pleasure to make presents for all your family and friends.*

**Gifts for every occasion**
Whether it is a birthday, christening, wedding or Christmas, a handmade gift will be remembered and treasured long after store bought items have been forgotten. When you are creating a gift with a special recipient in mind, it is easy to take their personality and preferences into account and come up with a truly appropriate and personal present.

**For you and your home**
While your friends are clamouring for the beautiful and unique gifts you are creating, don't forget to save some time to make something special for yourself and for your home. Not only will you save money but you will be able to give your home a very attractive coordinated look with matching cushions, decorations and table linen.

**All the family**
You will discover that once you begin to create a host of desirable gifts, other members of the family will want to join in. Children can help with many of these

projects and they will learn new skills as well as producing presents that grandparents and other relatives will treasure for ever!

**Ideas and advice**
This book will inspire and guide you through over 60 projects. Included in this book you will find:

* A photograph showing the finished result for every project. This will help you to choose appropriate presents and complete them successfully.

* A list of exactly what materials you will need for each project, followed by simple step by step instructions that guide you from start to finish.

* Clear diagrams amplifying the instructions wherever necessary so you can see exactly how an item is made.

* Useful tips to help you avoid the pitfalls and obtain a really professional result.

* A stunning selection of simple projects that take a minimum of time and money to complete, allowing beginners to get satisfactory results straightaway and for more experienced crafters to extend their skills.

* Inspiration to develop your own craft ideas and skills. You can expand and develop many of the projects to give them your very own personal touch.

> Please note that many glues contain substances that can be dangerous if inhaled. Glue should be used in a well-ventilated room, and should be used by children ONLY under close adult supervision.

## PART ONE
### FRAGRANT GIFTS AND KEEPSAKES
Pot pourri, essential oils, lavender and other sweet-smelling herbs, are used in a delightful variety of projects to create gifts to suit all occasions. A wide variety of simple craft skills are employed including paper crafts, needle crafts and nature crafts using dried flowers and grasses.

## PART TWO
### SEWN FOR THE HOME
Taking the trouble to make a gift specially designed to suit a friend or relative's house or garden shows that you really care. If you are nervous about your sewing skills, you need not be. All the projects are easy to complete and have clear instructions. In no time you will be in demand to add those special finishing touches to the homes of your friends and neighbours.

## PART THREE
### FOR BABIES AND CHILDREN
Children have so many store bought toys today that it is really appreciated by parents and children alike when you give a gift you have made yourself. You will find ideal presents for parents-to-be just setting up a nursery and for birth and christening gifts. And when the birthdays begin to roll around, you will be able to create toys that are sure to become lasting family favourites.

## PART FOUR
### BETTER TECHNIQUES
Improve your skills with the simple advice and tips in this section, and you will soon be able to devise and make your own projects and personalize them to suit the recipient.

PART ONE

# *Fragrant Gifts and Keepsakes*

# Introduction to Part One

*From ancient times, aromatic potions and oils have been added to gifts to make them more pleasing. Here this charming old custom is revived for modern times.*

People have enjoyed using perfume in their everyday lives since the dawn of civilization.

In days when personal hygiene and sanitation were not as highly considered as they are now, fragrant oils and essences were a very important part of life for those who could afford them. Certainly they were used by the Greeks, Romans and Egyptians and it was quite a common custom for sweet-smelling rose petals and herbs to be strewn on to the paths of processions, when the air must have been heady with crushed, mingled fragrances. Perhaps this is where the modern tradition of scattering rose petals at wedding parties originated.

Cleopatra loved perfumes and must have spent her life drifting about on a cloud of it. To this day she is remembered for her exotic habit of bathing in scented oils.

No doubt her love of perfume did not go unnoticed by courtiers and servants wishing to gain favour.

## More recent times

As recently as the fifteenth century, posies and pomanders filled with herbs were carried by noblemen and women to help mask foul odours, and layers of lavender and other herbs were placed between stored gowns and cloaks to prevent moth and to sweeten the garments. Every large house had its own herb garden for medicinal and cosmetic use and plants were gathered and made into soaps, creams and sometimes candles.

By the eighteenth century, manufactured perfumes were being sold all over Europe and though the old country fragrances were still made at home (Carmelite nuns used to make fragrant waters), they were not as necessary as they had been.

## Fragrances for today

Nowadays, unwrapping a scented present gives the receiver added pleasure. It may be a beautifully-presented bowl of fragrant pot pourri, bringing into the

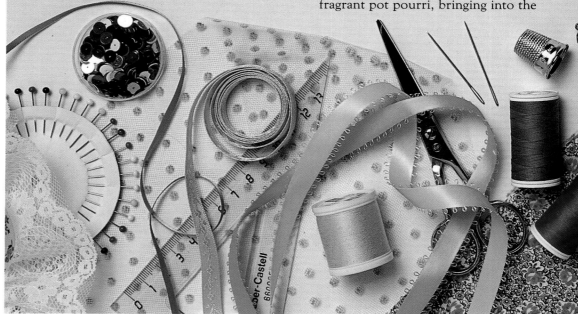

house all the lovely aromas of a spring garden or a dried flower arrangement with the spicey tang of a woodland walk redolent of the scent of moss, pine and citrus. A pillow containing the elusive reminder of rain-washed roses and sweet carnations cannot fail to please. There are many varied and unusual ways of making and giving scented gifts, most of them very simple.

Some perfumes you give may have been forgotten for years and their arrival will often evoke nostalgic memories.

Natural herbs, spices and flowers can be used to great effect; gifts can be designed for pretty and often practical purposes throughout the house. Linen bags and sachets, padded coat hangers, sleep pillows and cushions filled with hidden perfume will all give a delightful ambience to a room.

Try making herb garlands and mixtures of dried flowers and herbs which will keep insects at bay in the kitchen. Make a special statement for a birthday or wedding party with miniature arrangements of scented flowers or bridesmaids' gifts.

For a little girl, what could be prettier than a perfumed lavender lady doll or a dainty basket of tiny scented flowers? Flower pomanders and lace sachets are romantic gifts for a wedding, as are a lacey perfumed garter and a drawstring bag made to match the bride's gown. The bridesmaids will like one too!

Bowls of pot pourri, perfumed notepaper, greetings cards, wrapping paper and even scented inks are easy but effective gifts which will remind people of the care you took to create a special and very individual gift.

**Essential oils**

It will repay you to investigate the whole range of essential oils available.

A basket of pine cones with a few drops of essential oil added and placed by the fire, soon permeates the room with lovely woodland smells.

Some can be added to pot pourri recipes to give an invigorating and refreshing smell, while others have more relaxing, soporific qualities.

You will soon discover new ways of making and presenting scented gifts to create an atmosphere of romance or nostalgia, or merely as fun for your friends. These suggestions and ideas are bound to help you to make your gifts doubly welcome.

In the instructions, the specific materials you will need to make each item are listed, but not the basic materials needed for any craft work, such as scissors, needles and thread. If any unusual materials are required, they will be listed.

# Flower collage

*A dainty dressing table gift made of small dried flowers, carefully stuck in a heart-shaped picture frame and brushed with essential rose oils to give lasting fragrance.*

## Materials
3 × 3in (7.5 × 7.5cm) heart-shaped picture frame
White card to fit inside frame
All-purpose adhesive
Dried deep pink rosebud
Dried blue larkspur flowers
Dried pink larkspur flowers
Dried white statice flowers
Dried pale green grasses
Rose oil

## Preparation
1  Remove the backing from the picture frame and discard the front glass. Measure and cut the card to fit snugly inside the frame.

2  Draw a light pencil line all round the card to mark the edge of the frame.

3  Draw a cross on the heart from side to side and from top to bottom, to mark the centre of the card.

4  Sort out the dried material, choosing the smallest flowers and grasses. Trim off the stalks to make a flat surface for easier sticking.

5  Brush a thin layer of adhesive on to the card.

## Vary the design
You can use different colours to vary the design. A dried daisy in the centre, for example, could be surrounded with gold and amber coloured flowers, then brushed with sandalwood oil.

## Working the design
6  Trim off the stalk of the dried rosebud, add a dab of adhesive and press it firmly on to the middle of the card.

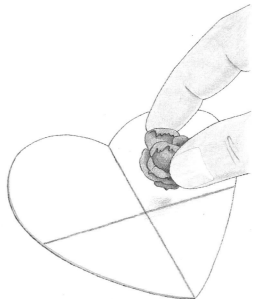

Centring the rosebud.

7  Choosing small flowers, press a circle of dried blue larkspur round the rosebud, making sure the flowers are attached firmly. Follow with a half circle of pink larkspur flowers.

8  On top of the heart, press on some white statice and a few grass seeds to complete the heart design. Do not place any flowers beyond the outline pencil mark. Allow to dry.

9  Very carefully, place the completed heart in the frame, making sure it is positioned centrally. Snap on the backing, then brush the rosebud with rose oil to give it lasting perfume.

# Sachets

*Quick to sew sachets filled with pot pourri or lavender make a charming little gift. Choose between round, square or heart-shaped.*

**Materials**
(For one round sachet)
Two 4in (10cm)-diameter circles of fabric
24 × ½in (61cm × 13mm) wide lace
Pot pourri
12in (30.5cm) bead trim

**To make the sachet**
1 With right sides together and taking a ¼in (6mm) seam allowance, baste and machine-stitch round the outside of the circles, leaving a small opening for filling.

2 Turn right sides out. Baste a lace frill round the outside edge of the circles, including the opening.

3 Fill the sachet with pot pourri. Hand sew the opening to close it, then continue sewing the lace frill all the way round the circle. Remove the basting stitches.

4 Sew on bead trim.

**Materials**
(For one plain sachet)
8½ × 3in (21.5 × 7cm) fabric
Pot pourri

**Preparation**
1 With right sides facing, fold fabric in half to form a shape 4¼ × 5in (11 × 12.5cm). Taking a ¼in (6mm) seam allowance, machine-stitch along the two longer sides.

A heart-shaped sachet.    Scale: 1sq = ½in (1.2cm)

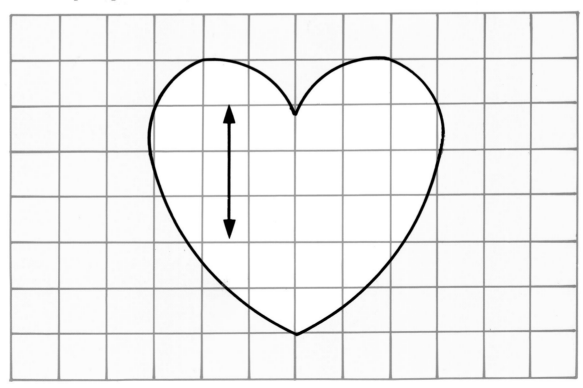

**2** Turn right sides out and fill with pot pourri.

**3** Sew the open end securely.

### Materials
(For one heart-shaped sachet)
Two 4 × 4in (10 × 10cm) fabric pieces
4ins (10cm)-wide length of lace
⅛in (3mm)-wide length of satin ribbon
Pot pourri

### Preparation
**1** Draw the graph pattern on squared pattern paper. Cut out the pattern piece. Pin to the fabric and cut out two pieces.

### Working the design
**2** With right sides together and taking a ¼in (6mm) seam allowance, baste and machine-stitch the sides together. Leave a small opening at the top of the heart. Turn right sides out.

**3** Baste a lace frill round the outside edge of the heart, including the top of the heart. Fill the heart with pot pourri.

**4** Hand-sew the opening to close it, then continue sewing the lace frill all the way round the heart. Remove the basting stitches.

**5** Make satin bows and sew them on to the front of the heart.

# Decorated straw hat

*This traditional-style straw hat will make a delightful gift – or an unusual wall hanging. Decorated with dried flowers, it has the added novelty of a hidden scent.*

**Materials**
A medium-sized straw hat
36 × 5in (91.5 × 12cm) lace ribbon
12 × 2½in (30.5 × 6cm) satin ribbon
All purpose adhesive
Dried blue larkspur flowers
Dried golden rod flowers
Dried pale green grasses
Small sachet of pot pourri

**Preparation**
1  Cut off the flower heads and work out the design.

2  Attach the sachet of pot pourri to the inside of the straw hat, sticking it on firmly.

**Working the design**
3  Fold the lace ribbon in half widthways and stick the folded end to the back of the hat to form a double streamer. Cut the ends of the streamer diagonally. Make a bow of satin ribbon and stick that on top of the lace ribbon at the point where the crown meets the brim of the hat.

4  Spread adhesive in a small circle on top of the hat. Press larkspur flowers firmly on the adhesive circle, followed by a small circle of separate golden rod flowers. Stick a thick layer of larkspur flowers around the base of the crown, adding a double layer on the front brim of the hat.

5  Stick a small cluster of golden rod and larkspur flowers on either side of the brim. At the back of the hat on either side of the lace streamer, stick grasses, golden rod and larkspur in a fan shape.

6  Stick a small line of larkspur down the centre of the lace ribbon from the brim of the hat to about half way down the length of the lace ribbon.

By changing the flowers on the hat and also the pot pourri mixture, you can create a completely different mood. For a romantic design, use roses and lavender heads with pink grasses, decorated with pale pink ribbon.

Decorating a straw hat.

16

# Basket of small dried flowers

*This pretty arrangement of tiny flowers is easy to make but very effective. Use a basket like this to decorate a bedroom or as a present for a small girl.*

## Materials
Small pink basket
Florist's dry foam
Small dried pink helichrysum
Dried statice
Small dried rosebuds
Dried sea lavender
Dried alchemilla
Several 5in (12.5cm)-long narrow pink
    ribbons in coordinated shades
Patchouli oil

## Preparation
1 Take time to select only the very smallest flowers, snipping the tips off the sea lavender and taking only dainty pieces of statice.

2 Shape a piece of florist's dry foam and fit it firmly into the basket, making sure it does not slip about.

## Working the design
3 Starting at the centre of the basket, push small pieces of helichrysum in to the foam.

4 Push small pieces of statice in to the foam round the edge of the basket.

5 Follow with the other flowers, forming an even dome shape. Work until the florist's foam is completely hidden.

6 Remember to push some flowers very close in to the foam and others less far in, as this will give more interest and movement to the arrangement.

7 Make a double bow of ribbons and attach it to the handle of the basket. Leave the ribbon ends hanging freely.

8 Perfume the flowers with a few drops of patchouli oil.

Basket of small
dried flowers

Many differently-shaped baskets can be found in florist's shops, each one presenting a challenge for the arranger, but if you are unable to find a basket easily, a prettily-shaped box or bowl will make an attractive substitute.

# Shell with dried flowers

*Capture the beauty of foam-capped waves with a shell from the sea shore, filled with dried flowers. Add some fragrant oil and use it as a bathroom decoration.*

**Materials**
Sea shell
Florists' dry foam
Cotton wool
Lavender oil
Dried green grasses
Dried sea lavender
Dried pink delphinium
Dried deep pink corn heads

**Preparation**
1 It is important to choose flowers that are evocative of the sea and shore. Look for those that are varied in shape and have interesting colours and movement.

2 Shape a piece of florist's foam to fit in to the cavity of the shell.

3 Make a small plug of cotton wool and press it firmly in to the shell cavity alongside the foam. Drop lavender oil on to the cotton wool.

4 Start the arrangement by pushing pieces of grass and sea lavender in to the foam, to make a pleasing outline.

5 Try to achieve a wave-shaped design by letting the flowers flow freely from the shell.

6 Arrange the rest of the flowers, remembering to place the larger ones close to the centre of the shell.

There are many differently-shaped sea shells to choose from. Some are spikey like the one shown here, others are quite smooth. Their colours will vary from soft pinks and browns to pale purples and white or cream. All purple, cream and blue flowers would go well with most shells.

A group of dried flowers arranged in shells would make an unusual table or sideboard decoration suitable for a festive occasion.

A Christmas arrangement could be made using red flowers and green foliage with the addition of dried grasses sprayed with silver or gold paint.

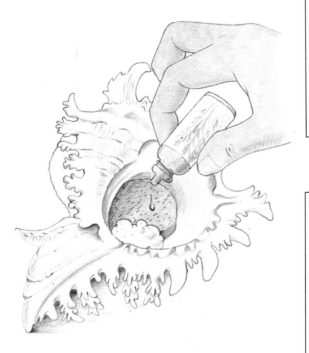

Adding perfume to the inside of the shell.

20

# Lavender lady

*This little 'granny' doll is bound to be a great favourite with small girls. She is easily made out of scraps of fabric and is filled with lavender.*

## Materials
6in (15cm)-diameter circle of flesh-
   coloured stockinette for the head
Two 1in (2.5cm)-diameter circles of flesh-
   coloured stockinette for hands
Polyester wadding
Red thread
Black thread
11in (28cm) thick white cotton thread
26 × ⅛in (66cm × 3mm) ribbon
19 × 10in (48 × 25.5cm) piece of lavender-
   coloured fabric for body
4½in (11.5cm)-diameter circle of lavender-
   coloured fabric
Dried lavender
4in (10cm)-diameter circle of card
35 × 7½in (89 × 19cm) piece of lavender-
   coloured fabric for skirt
130 × 1½in (330 × 3.5cm) lace
30 × 1in (76 × 2.5cm) lace
19 × 6½in (48 × 16.5cm) striped fabric for
   apron

## Preparation
**1** Sew running stitches round the outside of the head and hand circles, stuff with polyester wadding and draw up the stitches to form three ball shapes.

**2** Embroider two eyes in black and a mouth in red. Pencil in the eyebrows.

**3** Sew a tiny circle of stitches in the middle of the face and draw it into a circle with a small amount of wadding inside, to form a nose.

**4** Sew the strands of thick white cotton thread on the head with a line of stitches from the forehead to the nape of the neck, to make hair.

Stitching the nose.

Sewing on the hair.

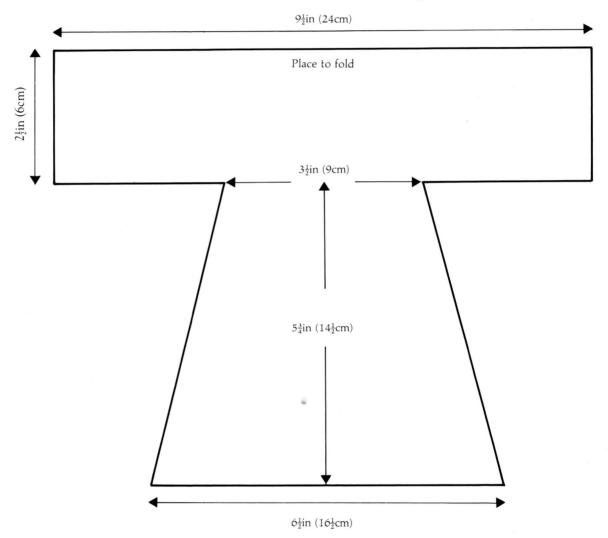

**5** Stitch the hair to the head at the ear points and draw in to two bunches on either side of the face.

**6** Plait the bunches and secure the ends of the plaits with ribbon.

**Working the design**

**7** Using the body pattern, cut out one piece of fabric. Fold the body pattern at the fold line and stitch round the edges taking a $\frac{1}{4}$in (6mm) seam allowance and leaving the base open.

**8** Fill the body with polyester wadding and a scattering of dried lavender.

9½in (24cm)

Place to fold

2½in (6cm)

3½in (9cm)

5¾in (14½cm)

6½in (16½cm)

Pattern dimensions for the body of the doll.

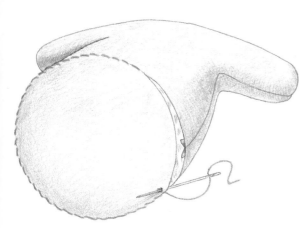

Sewing on the base of the doll.

**9** Oversew the lavender-coloured fabric circle with the card circle inside, to the base of the doll, tucking in the raw edges.

**10** Run a line of stitching round the ends of the arms and gather the stitching to form a wrist. Sew on the hands.

**11** Sew the head to the centre of the arms.

**12** Make the skirt by stitching the short ends of the rectangle together. Hem the bottom edge of the skirt. Gather up a length of 1½in (3.5cm) wide lace, baste it to the bottom hem, then stitch in place.

**13** Gather the skirt top by sewing running stitches round the top edge of the skirt. Draw the stitches up and fit the skirt tightly round the doll to form a waist.

**14** Make an apron by hemming two short and one long edge of the striped fabric. Gather up a length of 1½in (3.5cm) wide lace, baste it to the hems and stitch in place.

**15** Sew running stitches along the top edge of the apron. Draw the stitches up and fit the apron tightly round the waist on top of the skirt. Cover the gathers with a long length of 1in wide (2.5cm) lace tied in a bow at the back.

**16** Sew a length of 1in (2.5cm)-wide lace to go round the back of the doll and cross over the bodice. Gather small pieces of 1in (2.5cm)-wide lace and sew them to the neck and wrists.

**17** Make a tiny dolly bag out of two squares of striped fabric. With wrong sides of the fabric together, machine-stitch three sides and turn right sides out.

**18** Hem the open edge. Gather a length of 1in (2.5cm)-wide lace and sew it along the open edge. Fill with lavender, gather the open edge and tie a length of ribbon round the gather. Sew on a ribbon handle.

Make running stitches around the skirt top and pull threads to gather.

Make variations on the lavender lady by dressing the doll in different ways
  A fairy doll to go on the top of a Christmas tree could have yellow hair, a golden paper crown and be dressed in white silk and lace with sparkling wings made of gold cardboard. Characters from fairy tales and children's stories make excellent subjects for dolls.

# Writing paper and ink

*Sending or receiving a letter written on perfumed note paper makes the occasion a special one. If you add some scented ink, it will be a romantic gift.*

## Materials
Good quality writing paper
Envelopes
Sachet of pot pourri

## Preparation
**1** Choose a really pretty notepaper. Often this can be bought in an attractive presentation box. Remove any wrapping.

**2** Place the paper in a large plastic bag with a sachet of prepared pot pourri to perfume it, for two to three weeks.

Alternatively, you could place a small sachet of pot pourri inside the box of notepaper before offering it as a present.

To scent ink, simply pour a few drops of oil of lavender or rosemary in to a bottle of ink. Stir it and replace the cap tightly.

## Covering a domed box
The box in the picture was professionally covered, but it is not difficult to cover such a box yourself. All you need is a plain box, wrapping paper and wallpaper paste.

Draw a box outline like the one in the diagram to fit the box, and cut the shape out of wrapping paper.

To ensure that there are no wrinkles, dampen the wrapping paper before sticking it.

Stick bottom and sides first, pressing down all the tabs, then stick the front and back plus dome and stick all tabs.

Finally, stick the inside strip and smooth down the paper with a clean, dry cloth to remove wrinkles.

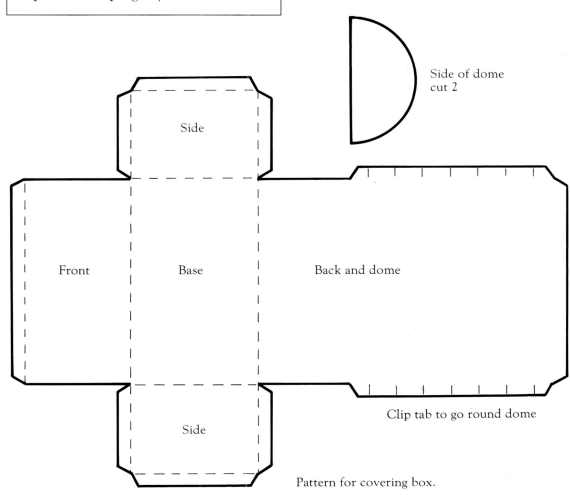

Pattern for covering box.

# Greetings tags

*It is delightful to receive a prettily wrapped-present with a perfumed greetings tag attached to it. 3D decoupage is a simple and effective decorative technique.*

## Materials
Three or four identical motifs from giftwrap, posters or notepaper
Stiff paper or thin card for base
Hole puncher
Spray adhesive
Double sided adhesive pads
Metallic thread
Small manicure scissors with curved blades
Sachet of pot pourri

## Preparation
1 Use the small scissors to cut out one complete design motif. Fold the stiff paper or card in half. Mount the motif on the card with spray adhesive, positioning the left hand edge of the motif against the fold.

2 Carefully cut around the motif, making sure the fold is not cut away. Open out the card and use the hole puncher to make a hole in the top left hand corner of what will be the back of the card.

## Working the design
3 Cover the whole motif with sticky pads, cutting them down to size as necessary. Avoid placing them at the edge of the design where they may show. Cut out another complete motif and position this accurately over the sticky pads.

4 Look at your chosen motif and decide which areas you want to lift forward. Bear in mind that the aim is to lift the subject matter in the foreground closer, so that details which appear closest to you in the picture will be the top layer of your design. Place sticky pads over your selected areas, and cut out the relevant

details from the third motif. Stick these over the pads.

5 Continue adding sticky pads to the chosen areas and cut more details from the fourth motif. Position over the pads.

6 Cut a short length of metallic thread and slip through the hole in the card. Tie the ends together and trim.

7 Place the gift tags in a plastic bag with a sachet of pot pourri to perfume them, for two to three weeks.

Cover the motif with sticky pads.

Add more pads to the projecting areas.

28

# Paper fan

*Fans were once an essential part of the fashionable woman's wardrobe, with a language of their own. You can make an attractive modern fan out of paper.*

## Materials
12 × 18in (30.5 × 46cm) piece of good
    quality gift wrapping paper
Spray mount adhesive
12 × 18in (30.5 × 46cm) piece of cartridge
    paper
36 × ⅝in (91.5cm × 16mm) ribbon
All-purpose adhesive
Sachet of pot pourri

## Preparation
1 Spray the back of the wrapping paper with the spray mount adhesive and stick it to the cartridge paper.

2 On the back of the cartridge paper, mark and score lines 1in (2.5cm) apart across the width.

## Working the design
3 Fold the paper concertina-fashion along the score lines.

4 With the paper folded, cut the top in to a curved shape through all layers. This will give a scalloped edge to the fan.

5 Bind the folded paper with a short length of ribbon 4in (10cm) from the bottom, securing the ends of the ribbon with all-purpose adhesive. Open out the rest of the fan.

6 Make a long-tailed bow with the remaining ribbon and sew it to the securing ribbon at the front of the fan.

7 Place a small sachet of pot pourri inside the box in which you are presenting the fan, to perfume it.

> Variations on the folded paper fan could be made by sticking thin lace on to coloured cartridge paper, by stencilling your own design on paper or by making a collage out of different pictures and sticking them on to cartridge paper, then folding.

Front

Cutting the top of the fan.

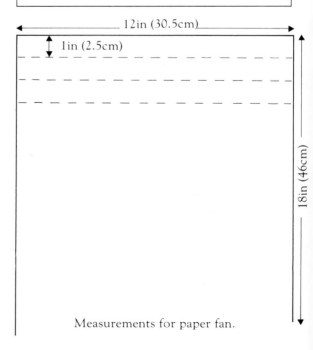

12in (30.5cm)

1in (2.5cm)

18in (46cm)

Measurements for paper fan.

# Book markers

*Book marker gifts would be suitable for children to try, with a little adult guidance. Choose coloured cards and decorate with pressed flowers or leaves.*

## Materials
7 × 2in (17.5 × 5cm) piece of coloured
   card
Pressed flowers, leaves or grasses
All-purpose adhesive
Hole puncher
⅛in (3mm)-wide Ribbon
Sachet of pot pourri

## Preparation
1  Trim the corners of both the top and bottom of the card to make attractive angles.

2  Carefully position a pressed flower or leaf on the card. When satisfied with its position, fix it in place with a dab or two of glue.

3  Punch a hole in the bottom of the card and thread a ribbon through the hole.

4  Place the book marker flat in a plastic bag with a sachet of pot pourri for a few days, to perfume it.

For a more ambitious project, make a flower collage of pressed flowers and leaves to create an all-over design. You can either finish the book marker with clear varnish to protect the dried material or cover it with the clear plastic film used for covering books, which is obtainable from stationers and art shops.

Choose ribbons in shades which will tone with the card.

Another idea is to cut lengths of pretty ribbon to book marker length. Trim them top and bottom. Sew a few beads on the top to make them even more decorative.

Make a number of cards and keep them in their scented plastic bag, ready to slip in to a gift.

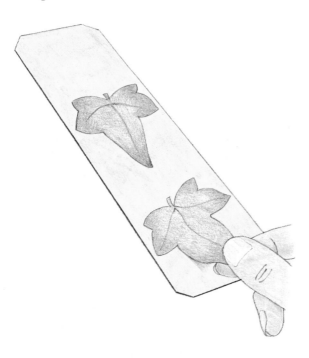

Positioning a leaf on a card.

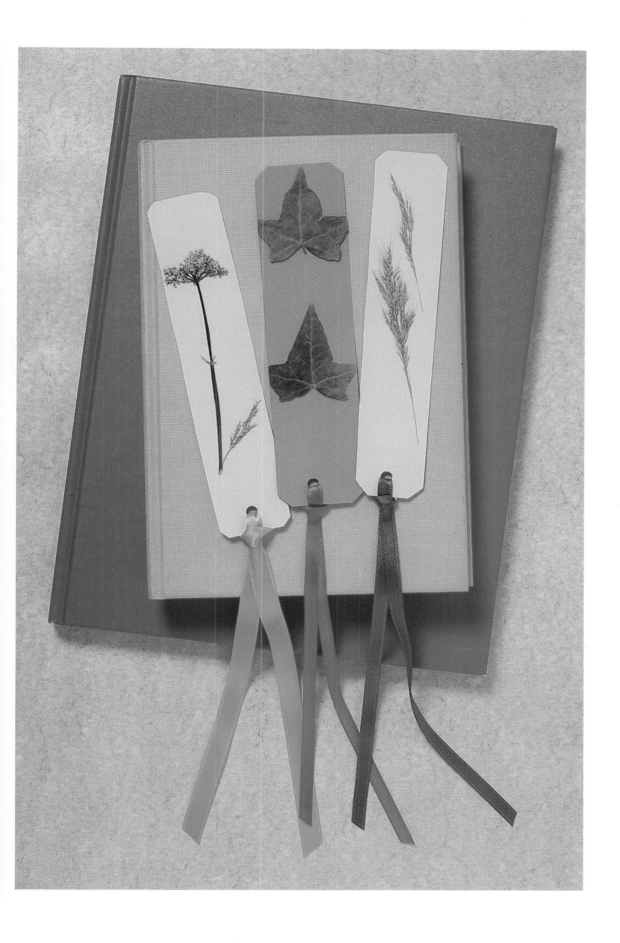

# Relax pillow

*Beautiful bed linen makes a perfect gift and a comfortable scented pillow is particularly good for busy people. This one is scented with relaxing pot pourri.*

## Materials

16 × 16in (40.5 × 40cm) patterned cotton fabric
16 × 16in (40.5 × 40cm) contrasting cotton fabric for backing
Ready-made cotton pad, to fit
Sachet of pot pourri

## Preparation

**1** Make a small slit in the cover of the cushion pad and sew in a sachet of pot pourri. Sew up the slit.

## Working the design

**2** With right sides together, machine-stitch the cotton fabrics, taking a 1in (2.5cm) seam allowance.

**3** Stitch round three sides of the square leaving an opening on the fourth side. Press the seams flat.

Make a small slit in the cover of the cushion pad.

**4** Turn right sides out and press again. Slip in the cushion pad and sew up the opening.

> If you wish, a small zip can be incorporated in to the back of the pillow so that the cover can be removed for laundering. Leave an opening large enough for the cushion pad to be inserted easily. The opening should come within 1in (2.5cm) of the two top or bottom corners at the back of the pillow.

> A pretty white cotton sleep pillow of the same size could also be made, decorated with broderie anglaise lace. Scatter in some pot pourri after filling the case with a fire-retardant, polyester stuffing insert.
>
> A pillow like this could also serve as a ring-pillow for a wedding.

# Catmint mouse

*Cats love the smell of catmint and are often to be found lying in a bed of it on a warm day. Make this fun mouse filled with the herb for your special cat.*

**Materials**
Two 8 × 5in (20 × 12.5cm) pieces of velvet or felt fabric
Dried catmint (*Napela cataria*)
10in (25.5 cm) narrow ribbon

**Preparation**
**1** Draw a pattern from the graph pattern on squared paper and cut it out. Pin the pattern to the fabric and cut out two shapes.

**2** With right sides together, pin the two shapes together, allowing a ¼in (6mm) seam allowance.

**3** Machine-stitch round the mouse, leaving a small gap underneath for filling.

**4** Turn right sides out.

**5** Fill the mouse with dried catmint. Sew a ribbon on securely to make a long tail. Sew up the opening.

**6** Embroider whiskers, eyes and nose in black cotton.

> Do not use any sharp-edged buttons or beads as these could harm a cat if it chewed them, as it probably will. It is safer to use only soft materials and to embroider the features of the mouse.

> Wormwood herb is excellent for ridding house pets of fleas. Mix it in to a pot pourri with dried thyme, lemon balm and sage. Fill a small pillow with the mixture and sew it in to your pets' bedding. Insects may well beat a hasty retreat!

Template for a catmint mouse.

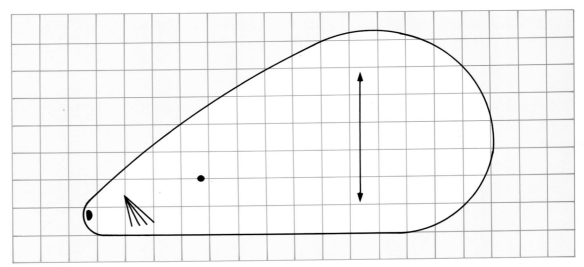

Scale: 1sq = ½in (1.2cm)

# Coat hangers

*Covered coat hangers make luxurious gifts. Here are two, a striped one for a man and a white one for a woman. Each is scented to keep clothes sweet-smelling.*

**Materials for striped hanger**
Wooden coat hanger
Tape
62 × ⅛in (155cm × 3mm) satin ribbon
All-purpose Adhesive
Polyester wadding
Pot pourri
24 × 7in (61 × 18cm) striped fabric

**Preparation**
1 Cover the hook with tape, then bind it tightly with satin ribbon. If necessary, stick the ends of the ribbon to hold them in place.

2 Cover the hanger with two layers of wadding, sprinkling pot pourri between the layers. Fold the ends in neatly and sew or stick the wadding along the edges to secure it.

3 On the wrong side of the fabric, baste a ¼in (6mm) wide double hem along the two long edges. Machine-stitch the hems and press them.

4 Find the centre of the fabric by folding it in half lengthwise, then folding it again, in four. Carefully cut a small hole in the centre of the folds for the hook to go through, by snipping off the corner.

**Working the design**
5 On the right side of the fabric, machine-stitch two lengths of ribbon lengthways along each side of the centre hole, ½in (13mm) from the outer edges.

6 With right sides of the fabric together, machine-stitch the two short edges together. Turn right sides out.

7 Slip the cover over the hook on to the hanger. Pin the two hemmed edges together, then sew them with running stitch, gathering the fabric as you go to take up the fullness.

8 Gather the top edge of the fabric with running stitch in the same way. Each end of the hanger should fit closely. Attach a satin ribbon bow.

**Materials for white hanger**
Wooden coat hanger
Tape
12 × ⅛in (30.5cm × 3mm) satin ribbon
All-purpose adhesive
Polyester wadding
Pot pourri
24 × 7ins (61 × 18cm) white fabric
Bead trimming
16 × 3in (41cm × 7.5cm) lace

**Preparation**
1 Follow steps 1 to 4 for the striped hanger.

2 Omit step 5.

**Working the design**
3 Repeat step 6.

4 Leaving about 2in (5cm) of lace for the centre trim, gather the rest of the lace to twice the length of the bottom of the hanger.

5 Slip the cover over the hook and on to the hanger. Pin the hemmed edges together with the lace frill doubled up between them, then sew with running stitch, gathering the fabric as you go to take up the fullness.

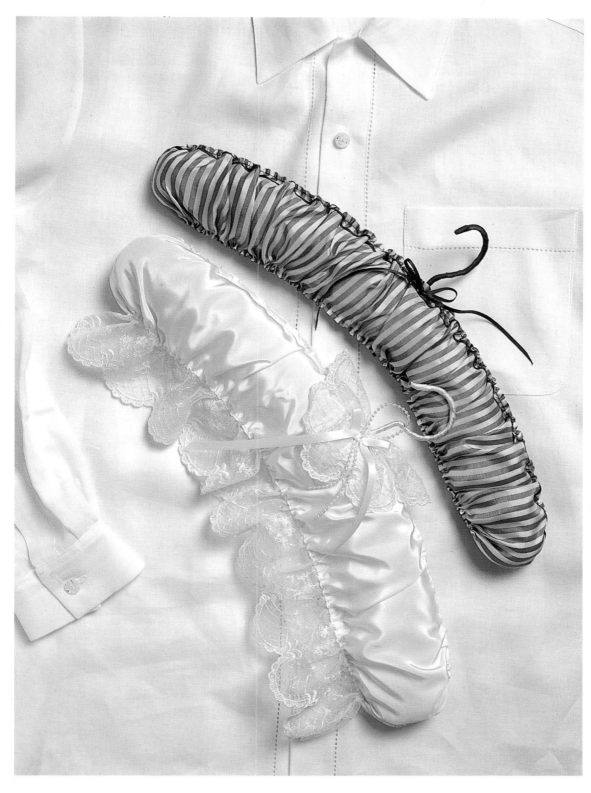

**6** Gather the top of the hanger with running stitch in the same way.

**7** Gather the short piece of lace so that it forms a circle. Sew it to secure the gathers, leaving a small hole, and slip it over the hook. Sew on the bead trim and a satin ribbon ribbon bow.

# Heart-shaped pincushion

*With the revival of interest in Victoriana, pincushions can make a romantic gift. A velvet heart with an initial picked out in pins gives this special appeal.*

**Materials**
Two 5½ × 6 (13.5 × 16.5cm) pieces of
    velvet
Polyester wadding
Pot pourri
Bead trimming
Dressmakers' pins
Beads
Sequins
Narrow satin ribbon

**Preparation**
1 Draw a pattern from the graph pattern on squared paper and cut it out. Pin to the fabric and cut out two hearts.

**Working the design**
2 With right sides together and leaving a ¼in (6mm) seam allowance, stitch round two sides of the heart, leaving a section open at the top for the filling.

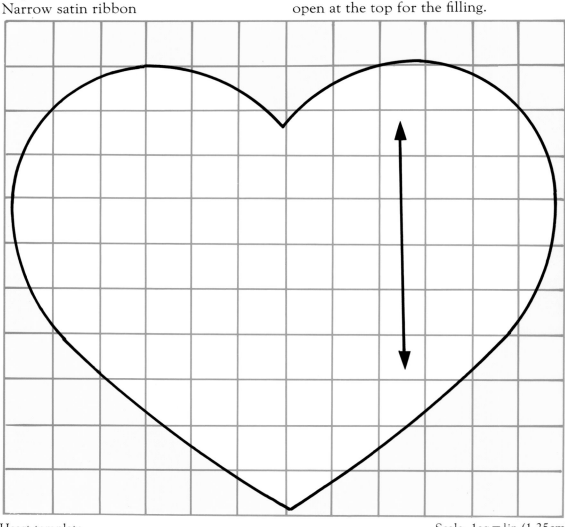

Heart template.

Scale: 1sq = ½in (1.25cm)

**3** Turn right sides out and fill with polyester wadding, adding some pot pourri.

**4** Sew up the open section of the heart and sew on the beaded trimming.

**5** Pick out an initial in beads secured by pins. Add other sequins and beads secured by pins. Trim with a satin ribbon bow and a bead tail.

# Nightdress and lingerie cases

*Add a touch of luxury to a bedroom with these pretty lacey cases. They would make beautiful gifts, particularly if they were scented with a soft fragrance.*

**Materials for nightdress case**
Two 30 × 13in (76.5 × 33cm) pieces of
 polyester cotton
28 × 1in (71 × 2.5cm) broderie anglaise
 eyelet ribbon
2yd × 3in (2m × 8cm) broderie anglaise
 frilling
Pot pourri
Polyester wadding
3yd × ⅛in (3m × 3mm) satin ribbon
18 × ½in (46 × 13mm) satin ribbon

**Preparation**
**1** Machine-stitch two rows of broderie anglaise eyelet ribbon, 3in (8cm) and 6in (15.5cm) from the top of the narrow edge of one piece of polyester cotton. Machine-stitch two tucks above and two tucks below the eyelet ribbons.

**2** Baste the broderie anglaise frill to the right side of the top edge and one third of the way down two long sides of the same piece of fabric with the frill facing the centre of the fabric.

**Working the design**
**3** With right sides together, place the second piece of fabric on top of the frill, so that it is sandwiched between the two pieces of polyester cotton.

**4** Sprinkle pot pourri on the top piece of polyester cotton and lay a piece of polyester wadding the same size on top.

**5** Leaving a ¼in (6mm) seam allowance, tack and then machine-stitch all round the edges, leaving a small gap at the bottom for turning.

**6** Turn right sides out. Sew up gap.

**7** Turn up the bottom half of the case to form an envelope. Sew in place. Press flat. Thread double ribbon through the eyelets. Finish both ends with bows.

**Materials for lingerie case**
96 × 3½in (240 × 9cm) lace
Two 10 × 30in (25 × 76cm) pieces of
 polyester satin
Pot pourri
Polyester wadding

**Preparation**
**1** Gather half the lace to make a frill and baste it to the right side of the top edge and down one third of two long sides of one of the pieces of satin, with the frill facing the centre of the fabric.

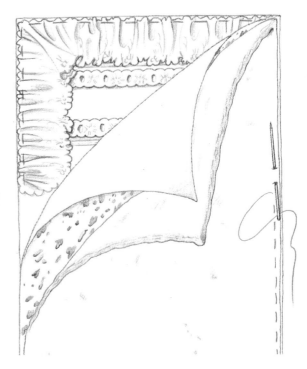

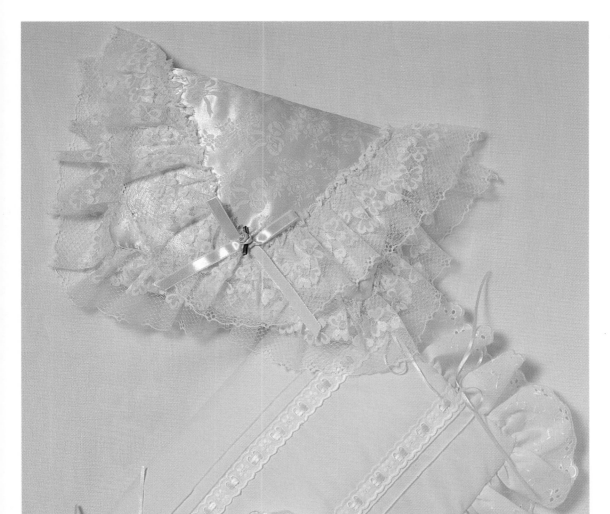

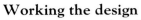

**Working the design**

**2** Follow steps 5 to 8 for the nightdress case.

**3** Gather the remaining half of the lace to make another frill and sew it in a V shape

to the front of the case. Decorate with a ribbon rose on a ribbon bow.

# Herb bags

*Crisp gingham bags filled with a sweet-smelling herb mixture of pot pourri will brighten up a kitchen and would make a very welcome house-warming gift.*

## Materials
Several 4½in (11.5cm) diameter circles of
  gingham fabric
Equal number 3½in (9cm) circles of
  muslin
Pinking shears
Pot pourri
Ribbon

## Preparation
1 Trim the edges of the gingham fabric circles with pinking shears.

2 Sew a line of running stitches around the edge of each circle. Do not make fast the ends of the thread.

## Working the design
3 Put a small scoop of the pot pourri in the centre of the muslin circles. Draw up the edges to form a small bag and secure it by sewing.

4 Place the muslin bags in the gingham circles and draw up the edges to make a bag. Secure the opening with ribbon.

Filling the inner muslin bag.

Several gingham bags in a pretty glass storage jar will make an acceptable gift. Here is a recipe for herb mix pot pourri:
1 cup of crushed peppermint leaves
1 cup of cologne mint leaves
1 cup of shredded bay leaves
1 cup of sage and rosemary leaves
1 teaspoon of powdered clove
1 teaspoon of mixed spice

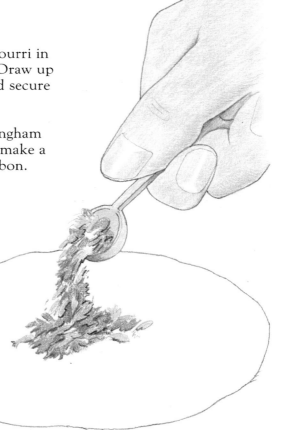

44

# Bridal bag

*This pretty drawstring bag could be a useful accessory for a bride to carry on her wedding day. Made of silk and lace, the fabric could match her gown.*

### Materials
15 × 5½in (38 × 14cm) lace
15 × 5½in (38 × 14cm) silk fabric
15 × ½in (38cm × 13mm) satin ribbon
5in (12.5cm)-diameter circle of silk fabric
   for the base
Sachet of pot pourri
36 × ¼in (91.5cm × 6mm) satin ribbon for
   drawstrings

### Preparation
1 Lay the lace on the right side of the silk fabric. Make a French seam down the narrow side of the fabric to form an open-ended tube. (This will hide the raw edges.)

### Working the design
2 Turn over one raw edge of the tube to make a seam on the right side of the fabric. Press.

3 Cut the ½in (13mm) satin ribbon in half to make two pieces 7½in (19cm) long.

4 Turn under the four narrow ends of the ribbons and machine-stitch the two lengths of ribbon on to the silk and lace tube so that they cover the raw edge of the seam on the right side. This will make a neat casing for the drawstring.

5 With right sides together, baste and then machine-stitch the circle of fabric to the bottom of the tube, forming a bag. Oversew or bind the seam to neaten it.

6 Sew a small sachet of pot pourri inside the bag.

Threading the ribbon through the casing.

7 Turn right sides out and thread two lengths of narrow ribbon through the ribbon casing. Sew the ends of the ribbons to make two continuous loops and pull them on either side of the bag to make ribbon drawstrings of even length.

This drawstring bag could be made out of any fabric, and it could be any size.
   It would make an excellent cosmetic bag or a useful sewing hold-all to take away on holiday filled with needles, thread, thimble and a small pair of scissors, all of which are handy in an emergency.

# Garter

*A scented garter is another lovely gift for a bride. This one is quite easy to make but the lace and satin make it look elaborate and glamorous.*

### Materials
30 × ½in (76cm × 13mm) satin ribbon
30 × 3in (76 × 7.5cm) lace
15½ × ¼in (39.5 × 6mm) elastic
1yd × ⅛in (1m × 3mm) satin ribbon for roses and bows
Bead trim
Sachet of pot pourri

### Preparation
**1** Stitch the ½in (13mm)-wide ribbon on to a length of lace ½in (13mm) down from the top. Stitch both edges of the ribbon.

### Working the design
**2** Thread the elastic through the ribbon, gathering up the lace as you go. Secure the ends of the elastic and the ribbon.

**3** Sew the ends of the elastic, ribbon and lace together to form a garter.

**4** Press with a cool iron.

**5** Trim with satin roses, bows and bead trim.

**6** Place in a bag with a sachet of pot pourri to perfume it.

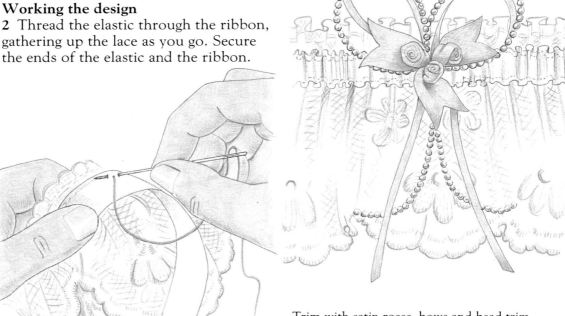

Trim with satin roses, bows and bead trim.

You could use narrow white or blue velvet ribbon instead of satin ribbon and trim the garter with tiny silk flowers.

Stitching ribbon to a length of lace.

# Flowers in eggshells

*A pretty basket containing eggshells filled with tiny posies of dried flowers will make a delightful and unusual gift to offer on an Easter morning.*

**Materials**
Bought rustic basket
Eggshells
Coloured tissue paper
Dried hydrangea
Dried yellow yarrow
Dried pink and red statice
Grasses
Carnation oil
22 gauge florist's wire

**Preparation**
**1** Wash and dry the egg shells. Cut them in half and trim the edges.

**2** Line the basket with tissue paper.

**3** Place the eggshells in the basket, arranging them so that the tissue paper cushions each shell.

Tuck short pieces of statice in the handle of the basket.

Wire stems to make tiny posies to fit in eggshells.

**Working the design**
**4** Snip short the stems of some of the flowers and wire them together to make tiny posies to fit in to the eggshells. Mix the colours to get a nice bright, natural effect.

**5** Tuck short pieces of statice in to the handle of the basket and round the edges to add some extra colour.

**6** Perfume the flowers with a few drops of carnation oil.

Another way of adding perfume to this arrangement of flowers in eggshells would be to tuck a sachet of pot pourri underneath the tissue paper lining.
  Either of the 'Rose dream' or 'Lavender time' pot pourri recipes would provide a suitable fragrance.

50

# Flower head mosaic

*A dried flower mosaic set in a decorative box makes this an unusual table centre. It is also delicately perfumed, and would make a delightful housewarming gift.*

### Materials
Hexagonal gift box
Florist's dry foam
Dried teazels
Dried rosemary, dyed blue
Dried gold yarrow
Dried love-in-a-mist
Dried pink and cream canary grass
Dried poppy heads
Dried white statice
Citronella oil

### Preparation
1 Cut a hexagonal piece of florist's dry foam to fit the gift box.

### Working the design
2 Cut a teazel so that the stem is 2in (5cm) long and insert it in to the centre of the foam.

3 Cut the rosemary so that it is 2in (5cm) long and insert it at the edge of the foam to make a border of rosemary inside the outer edge of the box. Pack the flowers closely together.

4 Following the diagram and starting at the edge next to the rosemary, insert yarrow, love-in-a-mist, canary grass and poppy heads, filling any spaces with white statice.

5 Aim to achieve an even, closely packed design with no gaps. You will soon see the mosaic pattern emerging.

6 Add a few drops of citronella oil to the teazel to perfume it.

Plan of flower mosaic.
R – Rosemary
L – Love-in-a-mist
CG – Canary grass
Y – Yarrow
P – Poppy heads
S – White statice

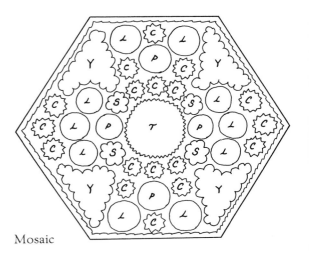

Mosaic

There are so many varieties of container to be found in the shops. Confectioners are particularly imaginative in their use of gift boxes, especially at Christmas time.

Save any pretty boxes you may be given. They always come in useful and it would be a charming idea to return one to the donor, filled with dried flowers!

52

# Dried flower posy

*Posies of aromatic flowers and herbs were popular in the past.*
*This posy of long lasting, perfumed dried flowers, could be*
*used on more than one occasion.*

### Materials
Dried cream helichrysum
Dried blue and yellow statice
Dried pink canary grass
Dried mauve sea lavender
22 gauge florist's wire
White stem tape
Silver wire
Cream and pink satin ribbon
Bought lace posy holder
Spotted net
Bergamot oil

### Preparation
1 Wire each of the flowers on to florist's wire and cover the wires with stem tape.

Bind the stems with tape.

### Working the design
2 Surround a piece of blue statice with five cream helichrysum flowers. Bind the stems together with silver wire.

3 Bind in the pink canary grass and yellow statice.

4 Continue placing and binding in the remainder of the flowers, aiming for a closely packed design. Finish with an outside circle of sea lavender and some cream ribbon bows.

5 Bind the stems with tape. Wind pink ribbon round the binding to cover it and slip the completed posy in the lace posy holder.

6 Make some ribbon bows and twist them on to wire so that they can nestle among the flowers in the holder. Make a spotted net bow to go round the bound stems.

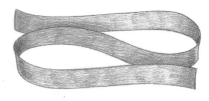

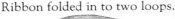

Ribbon folded in to two loops.

Twist wire round to secure.

7 Add a few drops of bergamot oil to the centre flowers.

# Herb garland

*The kitchen is often overlooked when it comes to making gifts but a garland of dried herbs on a gnarled twig would give a kitchen a fresh country look.*

**Materials**
Bought medium-sized twig wreath
Dried grasses
Dried sage
Dried rosemary
Dried wheat heads
Dried bay leaves
22 gauge florist's wire
1yd (1m) Ribbon
Green stem binding

**Preparation**
**1** Trim the dried material to make short, workable pieces.

**2** Wire pieces of grass, sage and rosemary in to small bunches.

**3** Wire wheat heads and bay leaves separately in twos and threes.

**4** Wire the ribbon in small bows.

**5** Bind all the wires with stem binding.

**Working the design**
**6** Aiming for a fairly loose, rustic style, insert the wired bunches of grass, sage, rosemary and wheat heads in the garland. Make all the herbs and grasses flow in the same direction.

**7** Secure the herbs to the garland with wire and stem binding.

**8** Continue round the garland leaving roughly 2ins (5cm) between each group of herbs.

**9** Fill in with the wired bay leaves and tuck in wired ribbon bows to finish.

Herbs and grasses should 'flow' in the same direction.

Garlands are particularly welcome at Christmas time, when their bright colours bring a note of gaiety to the festivities.
When making a Christmas wreath, it would be quite easy to tuck some sweet-smelling herbs among the holly and the ivy and let them add their fragrance to the house.

# Pine cone basket

*Pine cones arranged in an old fashioned basket are always a firm seasonal favourite. This particular basket has had a bow added to it for extra interest.*

**Materials**
Large basket
Pine cones
Helichrysum
Green fabric for basket lining
46 × 10in (117 × 25.5cm) piece of muslin
24 × 1½in (61 × 4cm) piece of muslin
Latex adhesive
20 gauge florists' wire
Pine oil

**Preparation**
1  Select, dry and clean pine cones and leave them to open their seeds in a warm, dry room.

2  Measure a piece of green fabric to fit inside the basket. Apply glue to the edges and fold over a small hem all round to neaten.

3  Line the basket with the prepared fabric.

**Working the design**
4  Arrange cones neatly in the basket on the green fabric.

5  Wire some small cones to the basket handle.

6  Arrange some helichrysum heads among the cones.

7  Make a muslin bow by folding the large piece of muslin in three lengthways and tie it in a floppy bow round the handle.

8  Tie the narrow strip of muslin to the opposite side of the handle.

9  Add a few drops of pine oil to the cones.

---

If you stand the basket near the fire, the pine perfume will fill the room with lovely fragrance.

---

58

# Pomander

*Pomanders were once carried by wealthy people to ward off sickness. Though they are no longer valued as a prophylactic, they make an aromatic gift for a friend.*

**Materials**
Tape
An orange
Pins
Knitting needle
Whole cloves with buds intact
Orris root powder
Ground cinnamon
Tissue paper
Ribbon

**Preparation**
1 Wind tape round the orange so that it is divided into four quarters. Pin the tape to the top and bottom of the orange and at the sides.

**Working the design**
2 Using the knitting needle and working one quarter at a time, pierce the skin of the fruit and insert the cloves in to the holes.

3 Follow the lines of the tape and insert cloves in lines until the skin is covered.

4 Mix orris root with the cinnamon. Roll the orange in the powder mixture and shake off the excess. (The powders will preserve the orange and give it a spicey fragrance.)

5 Wrap the orange in tissue paper and place it in a brown paper bag for three to five weeks in a warm, dry place. Allow the fruit to dry completely.

6 Remove the tape and replace it with ribbon. Make a hanging loop at the top by folding a length of ribbon and pinning it in place. As the fruit dries it will shrink. The spicey fragrance will last a long time.

You can also make a pomander out of a lemon. Wind the tape round the centre of the lemon only, then follow the instructions for the orange pomander.

Pomanders can be hung in clothes cupboards, where they will retain their pleasant smell for some time.

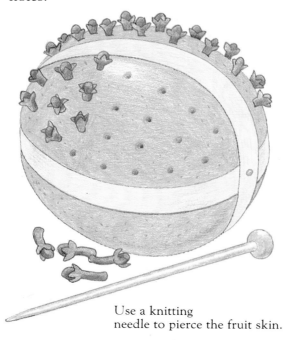

Use a knitting needle to pierce the fruit skin.

PART TWO

# *Sewn for the Home*

# Introduction to Part Two

*When something is handmade it is always extra-special, which is why sewing is not just a relaxing hobby providing hours of enjoyment, but is also a chance to create something personal.*

The projects included in this section have been specifically designed to appeal to a wide range of sewers – from busy mums who love to sew but lack time, to dedicated sewers looking for something new to make.

For the inexperienced or those whose time is at a premium, making things for their own home or to give to friends and neighbours, can provide just the right amount of sewing as well as adding those special finishing touches to the decor.

Even those with limited ability need not be daunted. The simple step-by-step instructions guide you through the construction from making the pattern to adding the final stitch. And, ever-conscious of time and tight budgets, each of the projects can be completed from start to finish in a short period of time, at a minimal cost.

The techniques described include many of the latest shortcuts and professional sewing tips. Gone are the days when sewing was a time-consuming chore; it really can be fun, quick and easy. And it couldn't be simpler; the materials required are listed at the beginning of each project. Many can be made from fabric remnants – it's worth raiding your work-box to find those treasured scraps that you refused to discard.

The Better Techniques, at the back of the book, include basic guidelines on equipment, stitching techniques, types of seam and seam finishes and other information that will help you acheive perfect results every time. If in doubt about any technique, take time to read this section before you begin, and so avoid any possible pitfalls.

All the measurements in this book have been expressed in both imperial and metric units. However the conversions used have been simplified and so are not exact. It is therefore advisable to follow one or the other of the measurement systems and not to mix them within a project.

With over 20 projects to choose from there is something for every occasion. Transform a room in minutes with the 30-minute cushions. The timely tote bag makes a great gift idea and the cook's apron can be made ready for the barbecue tonight!

Brighten up breakfast with the sunshine table set. The primary colours and painted faces will add a glimmer of cheer to the murkiest of mornings. Tiny tots are not forgotten and fun at playtime is ensured with the playmat. Pack a perfect picnic with the flowery picnic set and cutlery caddy.

Finally bring festive cheer to winter nights and count down to Christmas with our advent calendar. The holiday tablecloth has pockets in which to tuck hidden surprise presents.

Once started on the wonderful art of sewing for pleasure you will find the choices unlimited – a different fabric, change of appliqué or added embroidery will enable you to continue creating original gifts and new ideas for many years.

# 30-minute cushions

*Make either one of these comfortable cushions in a matter of minutes. Each one needs only a small amount of material so they are economical as well as speedy to sew.*

**Materials for bolster cushion**
½yd (50cm) of 36in (90cm) wide fabric
1⅛yd (1m) of ⅝in (1.5cm) wide ribbon
Bolster cushion pad

**Materials for square cushion**
⅝yd (60cm) of 54in (140cm) wide fabric
16in (40cm) square cushion pad

**Bolster cushion**
1  If necessary, cut the fabric to measure 20 × 36in (50 × 90cm). Then, turn both short ends under 4in (10cm), turning the raw edge under again ½in (1.25cm). Machine-stitch in place close to the turned edge and again 1in (2.5cm) from the first row to form the ribbon casing.

2  Fold the fabric in half lengthways, with right sides together and machine-stitch, leaving the ribbon casings free. To do this, stitch to the first casing, leave seam of casing section unstitched, stitch to the casing at the other end of the cushion cover, leave the casing free and then stitch to the end.

3  Press the seam and turn through to the right side. Cut the ribbon into two equal lengths and thread through the casings at either end. Finally, insert the bolster cushion before pulling the ribbon ties tightly, gathering each end. Finish with a firmly knotted bow.

**Square cushion**
1  Cut fabric to 21 × 46in (53 × 116cm). Neaten the short ends by turning under ½in (1cm) and then again, encasing the raw edges, and machine-stitching.

2  With right sides together, fold the ends to the centre and overlap by 4in (10cm) so that the overall width is 20in (50cm). Machine-stitch both side seams. Neaten and trim the raw edges and then turn through and press.

3  Finish with a machine-stitched decorative border 2in (5cm) from the outer edge all around the cushion cover.

NB: The overlapped edges should be sufficient to hold the cushion securely in place. However, a Velcro spot can be added to the centre back opening if desired.

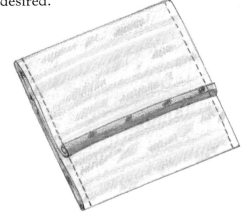

Overlap the ends, making the overall width 20in (50cm).

# Timely tote bag

*Lightweight but roomy, with a handy inside pocket, this timely tote will make a great gift. The wax-covered cotton is also waterproof, making it doubly useful.*

### Materials

¾yd (70cm) of 36in (90cm) wide waxed
  cotton fabric
5in (12cm) of Velcro

### Making the bag

**1** Fold the fabric in half, selvedge to selvedge with right sides together. Following the cutting layout cut 2 main pieces 15 × 17in (38 × 43cm); 2 facings 15 × 3in (38 × 8cm); 2 handles 3½ × 16in (9 × 41cm) and 1 pocket section placed on the fold 5in (13cm) square.

**2** Unfold the pocket section and then turn under ½in (1cm) at one end. On the wrong side machine-stitch one strip of Velcro over the turned edge. Stitch the other half of the Velcro to the wrong side of the other end of the pocket section ½in (1cm) from the raw edge.

**3** Fold the pocket so that the Velcro strips meet and there is a ½in (1cm) lip on the back of the pocket. Stitch the side seams (if using a fabric other than wax-covered cotton, stitch seams with right sides together and then turn through).

**4** Fold the handles in half lengthways, right sides together, machine-stitch the long edge and turn through. Then top stitch ¼in (6mm) from both side edges before pinning the ends of the handles to the top right side of the bag sections. Place them 4in (10cm) from the side edges and then machine-stitch in place.

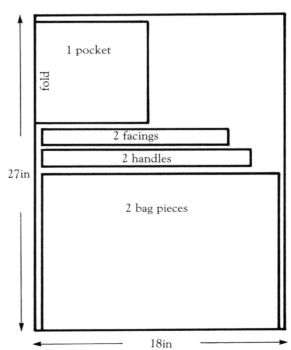

Fabric layout

**5** Pin the bag front to the back, with right sides together. Machine-stitch both side seams and across the bottom.

```
┌─────────────────────────┐
│░░░░░░░░░░░░░░░░░░░░░░░░░░░│
│   Velcro strip          │
│                         │
│  POCKET SECTION         │
│                         │
│   Velcro strip          │
│░░░░░░░░░░░░░░░░░░░░░░░░░░░│
└─────────────────────────┘
```

**6** Stitch the facings together end to end. Next, pin and stitch the facings to the top of the bag, right sides together and matching side seams with facing seams. Still working with the bag inside out, turn facings out to the wrong side of the bag, pressing the raw edges under ½in (1cm).

**7** Pin the pocket lip under the facing below one handle so that the top of the pocket with the Velcro closure butts up against the facing edge. Finally, top-stitch the facing to the bag close to the turned edge, catching the pocket lip as you go.

69

# Cook's cover apron

*This brightly coloured, no-nonsense apron is perfect for the busy cook, and accidental spills and splashes are easily wiped from the versatile chintz fabric.*

## Materials
¾yd (70cm) of 36in (90cm) wide cotton chintz or waxed cotton
2¼yd (2.10m) of 1in (2.5cm) wide grosgrain ribbon

## Making the apron

**1** Cut two rectangles for this basic shaped apron. The bib measures 10in (26cm) wide × 12in (30cm) deep and the skirt 26in (66cm) wide × 22in (56cm) deep. For the neck loop, ties and decorative trim, cut the ribbon as follows: neck loop 23 in (58cm) long; 2 waist ties, each 17in (43cm) long; 2 decorative trims, one 15in (38cm) and finally one 9in (23cm) long.

**2** Starting with the bib, hem either side edge by turning in ¼in (6mm) twice and machine-stitching. Fold one end under ½in (1cm), then a further 1½in (4cm) and pin in place. Then with the right side facing, machine-stitch this end with three rows of top stitching in a contrasting coloured thread.

**3** Next, join the bib to the skirt with the right sides together. Pin the unstitched edge of the bib to the centre of one long edge of the skirt. Machine-stitch 1in (2.5cm) from the edges. Open out the apron and press.

**4** With the wrong side facing, turn the seam allowance and remainder of top edge under ½in (1.25cm) twice and pin in place before machine-stitching right across from side edge to side edge.

**5** Pin the ribbon strips diagonally across the bottom left corner of the skirt, trimming the ends to match the side edges. Machine-stitch in place down either side of both ribbon trims. Then hem both side edges of the skirt encasing the ribbon ends at the same time.

Add three rows of machine top-stitch in a contrasting thread colour.

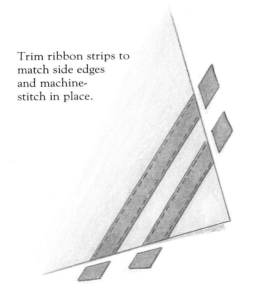

Trim ribbon strips to match side edges and machine-stitch in place.

**6** Finish the bottom edge by folding it under ½in (1.25cm), then a further 1½in (4cm). With the right side facing, top-stitch 4 rows of stitching in contrasting thread, approximately 1in (2.5cm) from the lower edge.

**7** Finally, add the ties and neck loop. Turn the ribbon ends under ¼in (6mm) and pin to the wrong side of the top edge of bib and either side edge. Machine-stitch, following the previous line of stitching and close to the outer edge.

# Sunshine table set

*Brighten the day with this sunny placemat and coaster table set.*
*Made from cotton, they are easily laundered so ideal*
*for everyday use at breakfast time.*

### Materials for six placemats
1⅛ yd (1.30m) of 36in (90cm) wide yellow
  cotton
Red, white and blue fabric remnants for
  face
6 yd (5.50m) orange bias binding
Orange and black thread
Interfacing
¾yd (70cm) of wadding

### Materials for six coasters
11in (28cm) of 36in (90cm) wide cotton
  poplin
11in (28cm) of 36in (90cm) wide white
  cotton poplin
Interfacing
For the face: fabric scraps and
  embroidery threads

### Making the placemats
1 Fold the yellow cotton in half
crossways. Draw around an upturned
plate or bowl, approximately 12in (30cm)
diameter, adding 2in (5cm) seam
allowances. Cut two pieces for each
placemat. Interface both sections. Cut
eyes and mouth from fabric remnants.

2 Bond the eyes and mouth to the right
side of one circle and zigzag-stitch around
the edges to secure in place. Using black
thread, add two French knots for the
nose and zigzag-stitch the eyebrows.

3 Quilt the back section of each
placemat (for quick and easy quilting, use
an interfacing with ready-printed quilting
lines such as Quiltex). Cut a circle of
wadding for each mat, again using the
plate as a template. Pin the wadding in
place over the quilted interfacing.

4 Add the appliquéd front, sandwiching
the wadding and with the face facing
uppermost. Machine-stitch through all
thicknesses all round. Trim the seam
allowance to within a scant ¼in (6mm) of
the stitching, clipping occasionally to aid
shaping.

5 Using bright orange thread, zigzag-
stitch the curved sun rays around the
edge, each approximately 1½in (4cm) long.
Finally, open out and pin the orange bias
binding around the edge, working with
the face side uppermost. Machine-stitch
in place and then turn the binding over
to the back, encasing the raw edges and
slipstitch in place.

### Making the coasters
1 To make the coasters, fold the fabric in
half in order to cut two layers at a time.
Using a large cup or saucer as a template,
draw around the cup, adding a further ½in
(1.25cm) seam allowance all the way
round. Cut 2 pieces for each coaster and
interface both layers.

2 For the face, cut the yawning mouth
from red poplin, bond in place and
secure with satin stitch. Add the
eyebrows, using a zigzag stitch and then
hand sew the eyelids and lashes. Finish
the face with two French knots to form
the nostrils.

3 Pin the plain circle to the face section,
with right sides together. Machine-stitch
½in (1.25cm) from the edge, leaving a
turning gap. Trim and clip the seam
allowance then turn through to right side.
Slipstitch the opening.

**4** Make the clouds from the white poplin. Again, fold the fabric in half so that the two layers are cut at the same time. Using tailor's chalk or a soft pencil, draw some cloud shapes. Cut two layers for each cloud, and interface both layers as before.

**5** Machine-stitch the two pieces with right sides together, turn through and press. Pin the cloud to the coaster on the left side and then top-stitch around the cloud edges attaching it to the coaster at the same time. Add some cloud shaping if desired, again by top-stitching.

# Napkins and rings

*These nifty napkins are quick and easy even for the complete novice. Made from squares of cotton, they are simply stitched and trimmed. Matching napkin rings add the finishing touch.*

**Materials for six napkins**
½yd (50cm) of 45in (115cm) wide yellow
  cotton
½yd (50cm) of 45in (115cm) wide white
  cotton
Yellow and white fabric paints

**Materials for six napkin rings**
Remnant of white cotton fabric
Remnant of yellow cotton fabric
Heavyweight interfacing
7½in (19cm) of ¾in (2cm) wide Velcro

**Making the napkins**
1  Cut three 15in (38cm) squares from
both pieces of cotton fabric. Fold each in
half and then into quarters.

2  Draw two scallop shapes on the outer
edge. Open out fabric.

3  Work a straight machine-stitch around
the scallop shapes, to prevent the fabric
from stretching, using white thread on
the yellow napkins and yellow thread on
the white. Then stitch again with a close
zigzag-stitch, going over the first line of
straight-stitching.

4  Using small embroidery scissors, trim
the napkin very close to the stitching
being careful not to cut the stitches. Press
the edges with a damp cloth.

5  Finish each napkin with a sleepy face
above one scallop. Draw lightly with
tailor's chalk or pencil and paint over
with fabric paint. Use white paint on the
yellow napkins and yellow paint on the
white.

**Making the napkin rings**
1  Using the template, cut 2 cloud pieces
for each napkin ring. Each cloud requires
a piece of fabric 4 × 8in (10 × 20cm).
From the yellow cotton fabric cut one
strip measuring 4in (10cm) wide × 7½in
(19cm) long for each ring.

2  Cut 1 piece of the heavyweight
interfacing for each cloud, again using the
template for size. Then for the rings, cut
a narrow strip 1½ × 6½in (4 × 17cm).

3  Fold the fabric strip in half lengthways,
with right sides together and stitch the
side seam. Refold the strip so that the
seam is in the middle and then place the
interfacing over the centre. Machine-
stitch across one end, catching the end of
the interfacing within the seam.

4  Turn the strip through to the right side
before tucking in approximately ½in
(1.25cm) of the unstitched ends to the
inside. Pin in place and press firmly.

Stitch Velcro to the cloud, and end of strip.

**5** For the cloud, pin the interfacing to the wrong side of one cloud piece. Add the remaining cloud section, sandwiching the interfacing. Machine-stitch around the edge using straight stitch. Then zigzag stitch over the edges all the way around to neaten.

**6** Machine-stitch the pinned end of a strip to the centre of each cloud base with the seam of the strip facing uppermost.

**7** With the cloud and attached strip still facing uppermost, cut a 1¼in (3cm) length of Velcro. Pin, then stitch, one half to the cloud just above the strip.

**8** To finish, turn the napkin ring over and stitch the remaining half of the Velcro to the opposite end of the strip. When completed, fold the strip over into a ring, so that the Velcro joins, and the ring sits on the cloud base.

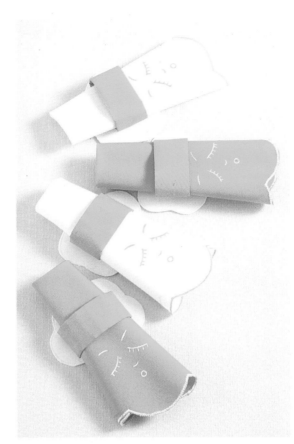

NAPKIN RING

# French bread bag

*Cook up an international flavour and keep delicious bread fresh for longer in this brightly-decorated French bread bag. It will add a splash of colour to any kitchen.*

## Materials
½yd (50cm) cotton chintz
20in (51cm) thick red cord
Remnants of red, white and blue cotton

## Making the bag
**1** Cut 2 pieces of cotton chintz measuring 26 × 7in (66 × 18cm). For the decorative flag, cut a strip 2¼ × 11in (6 × 28cm) each in red, blue and white cotton.

**2** Turn both long edges of each strip under ½in (1.25cm) and press to form crisp edge. Pin the red strip diagonally across the right side of one bag section, starting 1½in (4cm) from the bottom edge. Pin the white strip above this, overlapping the edges, and finally add the blue strip, again overlapping the edges. Machine-stitch in matching thread to hold in place, then trim the side edges of the strips to match the side edges of the bag.

**3** With the right sides together, pin the front to the back bag section. Starting at the top right side, machine-stitch for 3½in (9cm). Leave a 1in (2.5cm) gap unstitched for the cord casing, then continue down the side seam, across the diagonal strips to the end. Stitch the left side in the same manner, continuing across the bottom.

Position red strip first, then white above it, then the blue.

With right sides together, stitch back and front sections together.

**4** Turn the top edge under ½in (1.25cm) and press. Fold the top in again a further 2in (5cm) so that the pressed edge is just below the level of the gaps in the side seams and then machine-stitch in place. Machine a second row of stitching 1in (2.5cm) from the top edge to form the cord casing.

**5** Turn the bag to the right side and finish by threading the red cord through the casing.

# Cozy casserole coat

*Keep delicious dishes warm with this cozy casserole coat. The simple design can be adapted to any dish shape – making an attractive and practical addition to the dinner table.*

## Materials
¾yd (70cm) of 36in (90cm) wide medium-weight fabric *or* remnant to suit
Quilted interfacing or 4oz (200g) wadding

## Making the coat

**1** To measure the dish to determine the size of the coat required, first measure across the width of the base plus the height of the sides and then the length of the base including the height of the sides. Add ¾in (2cm) seam allowance to both measurements to determine the size of the coat pattern. Fold the fabric in half and cut 2 pieces to the size required. Cut a piece of quilted interfacing or wadding to the same size.

**2** To make the ties, cut 8 strips each 1 × 3in (2.5 × 7.5cm). With right sides together sew the long edge and across one end. Turn through to the right side and press.

**3** Lay the ties across the right side of one main piece, matching the raw edge to the side edge, 2in (5cm) from the corners so that each corner has two ties. Stitch in place and then fold all the ties to the centre of the main piece to prevent the loose ends catching in the side seams.

**4** Pin the wadding or quilted interfacing to the wrong side of the remaining back section and quilt in place. Then pin the back to the front with right sides together, sandwiching the ties.

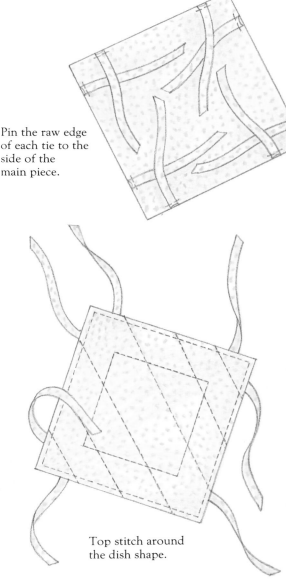

Pin the raw edge of each tie to the side of the main piece.

Top stitch around the dish shape.

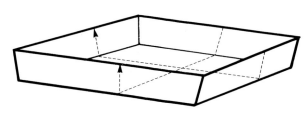

Measure width and length of dish, plus the sides.

**5** Machine-stitch the outer edge allowing $\frac{1}{2}$in (1.25cm) seam allowance, and leaving a small turning gap. Turn through, press and slipstitch the opening.

**6** Top-stitch $\frac{1}{2}$in (1.25cm) from the outer edge. Try the dish for size and lightly

mark the base area and then top-stitch around the dish shape to finish.

**7** Sit the dish in the centre and draw up the sides. Tie the corner strips together to form a loose cozy coat which will keep your casserole warm.

# Cherry pie pot holder

*This decorative pot holder will protect your hands from hot dishes and the pie crust top-stitching will ensure it holds its shape even after repeated laundering.*

**Materials**
2 × 11in (25cm) squares of cotton chintz and thermal lining
Remnants of red cotton and iron-on interfacing

**Making the holder**
1 Cut 2 circles of main fabric and 2 circles of heat-resistant thermal lining approximately 9in (23cm) in diameter (using a dinner plate as a template). Cut a strip for the hanging loop 6 × 1½in (15 × 4cm).

2 Make the cherry filling and appliqué cherries from a remnant of red cotton. Cut a triangular wedge 4½in (11cm) high × 4in (10cm) wide and two cherries, using a wine glass base as a template. Bond the cherry motifs to the right side of one main piece, positioning them just above the centre. Appliqué in position, adding white satin stitch highlights and green stems.

3 Prepare the pie filling wedge by interfacing the wrong side of the red triangle of fabric. On the right side draw the cherries using a small coin for size. Machine-stitch with black thread, adding white satin stitch highlights as desired.

4 Cut the wedge shape from the appliquéd circle of main fabric, 3½in (9.5cm) high × 2½in (6cm) wide allowing ½in (1cm) seam allowance. Machine-stitch the cherry filling in place, right sides together pivoting at top point. Neaten seams and clip close to the point before pressing the seams towards pie.

5 Fold the loop strip in half lengthways with right sides facing. Tuck the raw

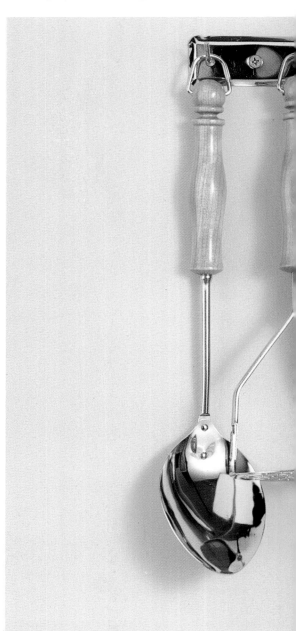

edges to the inside by $\frac{1}{2}$in (1.25cm), machine-stitch close to the edge and then press.

**6** Add the 2 circles of thermal lining to the wrong side of the appliquéd piece. Pin both ends of the loop to the top right side of the pot holder, matching raw edges. Pin the remaining circle of main fabric to the front, right sides together, sandwiching the loop.

**7** Machine-stitch through all layers, leaving a small 2in (5cm) turning gap. Neaten the seam allowance but leave it untrimmed.

**8** Turn the pot holder through and slipstitch the opening. Press. Top-stitch two rows of machine-stitching, around the pie crust, approximately $\frac{3}{4}$in (2cm) from the edge. Finish with short diagonal lines of stitching at regular intervals around the edge.

# Bread basket warmer

*Keep breakfast rolls and croissants warm in this cheerful warmer. The simple square design has bound edges with ties that form snug pockets in which to tuck the rolls and pastries.*

### Materials
Fabric remnant 17 × 34in (43 × 86cm)
Iron-on interfacing 17in (43cm) square
3yd (2.80m) bias binding

### Making the warmer

**1** Cut two 17in (43cm) squares from the fabric. Apply the interfacing to the wrong side of one fabric square, then pin the two fabric squares together with wrong sides together, sandwiching the interfacing.

**2** Open out and pin the bias binding around the edges of the joined squares. Machine-stitch in place before folding back over to the other side, encasing the raw edges. Pin in place.

**3** Cut the remaining length of bias binding into four equal lengths for the ties. Treating each tie in the same manner, fold under approximately ¼in (6mm) inside one end and then sew the end and side edges together. Pin the raw, unstitched end of each tie to a corner of the warmer, tucking the raw edges under the previously pinned bias binding.

**4** Once the ties are in place, top-stitch the bias binding edging close to the edge.

**5** To use the bread basket warmer, fold the four corners to the centre and press. Tie the diagonally opposite corner ties together in the centre.

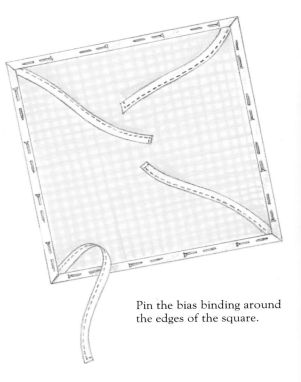

Pin the bias binding around the edges of the square.

Fold the four corners to the centre, over the bread.

# Garden chair cushions

*This stylish patio set of seat cushions will entice your guests to linger longer. Covered in reversible polka dot and spot, they can be turned to mix and match.*

## Materials

1½yd (1.40m) of 36in (90cm) wide polka dot cotton or chintz
1½yd (1.40m) of 36in (90cm) wide spot cotton or chintz
3yd (2.70m) of 4oz (100g) wadding
1⅜yd (1.30m) of 1in (2.5cm) wide elastic
4in (10cm) of 1in (2.5cm) wide Velcro
4 poppers

## Making the cushions

1 Cut a pattern piece for the back and seat cushions, the back to measure 10in (25cm) × 12½in (32cm) and the seat to measure 15in (38cm) × 13½in (34cm). Round off each of the four corners.

2 Fold the polka dot fabric in half and cut out 4 seat pieces and 4 back pieces. With fabric still folded cut out 4 back straps, tabs and loops as follows: 4 straps – 3 × 18in (8 × 46cm); 4 tabs – 3 × 1½in (8 × 4cm); 4 loops – 3 × 12½in (8 × 32cm).

3 Fold the spot fabric in half and cut out the remaining 4 back and seat pieces. Using the same pattern pieces, cut out 2 wadding pieces for each back and seat cushion. Cut the elastic into 4 even pieces.

4 For each seat cushion pin a polka dot to a spot piece, right sides together. Add two wadding pieces sandwiching the spotted fabrics in between. Machine-stitch around the edges through all thicknesses, leaving a turning gap in one edge. Trim the seam allowance and turn through. Slipstitch the opening. Press carefully.

5 Make each elasticated strap by folding the strap in half lengthways, stitch the side seam and refold to the middle. Insert the elastic, gathering the fabric to fit. Turn raw edges of one end to the right side of the strap and pin in place, then cover with a 1in (2.5cm) strip of Velcro, machine-stitched in place through all thicknesses. Pin the other end of the strap, with underside of strap facing the right side of a back piece, approximately 5in (13cm) from the top edge.

6 Make the short tab in the same manner as the strap, stitching the Velcro to the underside of the tab (over the seam). Pin to the opposite side of the back section, again with the underside of the tab facing the right side of the back and matching raw edges.

The elasticated strap passes through the vertical loop.

**7** Make the top loop by folding it in half lengthways and stitching the side seam and one end. Turn through and press. Pin the unstitched end to the right side of the back at the centre top edge.

**8** Pin the remaining back in place, with right sides together, sandwiching the strap, loop and tabs. Add the two layers of wadding, one either side, again

sandwiching the fabrics. Stitch around edges leaving a turning gap. Trim seams and turn through. Slipstitch opening.

**9** Try the back cushions on the chair backs adjusting the loop to the length required. Finish the loop with a popper to hold in place and so the cushions are easily removed or turned over when required.

# Fragrant flower picnic mat

*Enjoy balmy summer days and lunch al fresco with this colourful floral picnic mat. Each petal provides a place setting and the floral theme is further enhanced by the ladybird motif!*

## Materials

1yd (90cm) pale pink cotton poplin
1yd (90cm) rose pink cotton poplin
⅜yd (40cm) green cotton
⅜yd (40cm) yellow cotton
Iron-on interfacing
2 ladybird motifs

## Making the mat

1  Using the graph pattern, scale up and cut out 8 pale pink and 8 rose pink petals. Cut a further 8 pieces of iron-on interfacing and apply to four of each shade of petal.

2  Add a plain petal piece to each of the interfaced petal pieces with right sides together. Machine-stitch around the outer edge leaving the straight edge free. Trim seam close to the stitching, turn through and press.

3  Fold the green fabric in half lengthways and cut out 8 leaf pieces. Again interface four pieces before machine-stitching them to the four plain pieces, right sides together. Trim the seam allowance, turn through and press. Slipstitch the opening. Then top-stitch the leaf veins in a contrasting colour.

4  Layer the pink petals evenly in a circle, pin in place, leaving a hole in the centre. Add the leaves between every second petal and pin in place. Top-stitch around the outer edge of the petals and leaves, stitching through all thicknesses where applicable.

5  To add the centre of the flower cut 2 yellow 12in (30cm) diameter circles, using a dinner plate as a template. Interface both centre pieces and then turn the

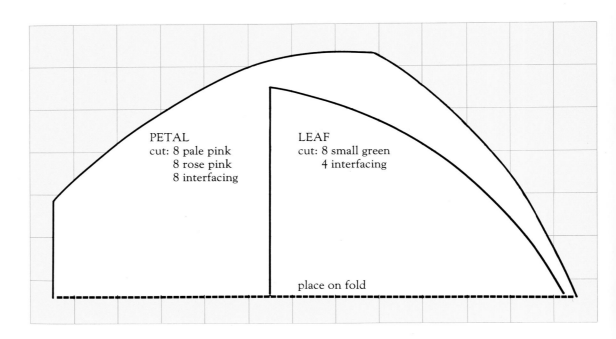

PETAL
cut: 8 pale pink
8 rose pink
8 interfacing

LEAF
cut: 8 small green
4 interfacing

place on fold

edges under approximately ½in (1cm), pressing in place as you go. Add random French knots for stamens to one centre piece and sew on the ladybird motifs as desired.

**6** Working with the right side facing, position the decorated centre circle in place, covering the petal edges. Machine stitch around the edges in matching thread. Turn the picnic mat over, trim the petal ends close to the stitching and press seam towards centre.

**7** Finish the underside by slipstitching the remaining yellow circle in place, covering the petal ends and the machine-stitching of the front centre piece.

# Picnic cutlery caddy

*This lightweight cutlery caddy holds six place settings plus condiments and napkins. The cord drawstring pulls together holding everything securely in place.*

**Materials**
1yd (90cm) of 54in (140cm) wide
   lightweight cotton fabric
26in (66cm) of 36in (90cm) wide
   interfacing
1yd (90cm) of cord

**Making the caddy**
**1** Cut one piece of fabric and interfacing for the caddy back 26 × 18in (66 × 46cm). Apply interfacing to the wrong side of the fabric and then fold the fabric in half with the right sides together. Machine-stitch the seam leaving a 4in (10cm) turning gap in the middle. Press the seam open and refold with the seam in the centre.

**2** Stitch across the top, taking $\frac{1}{2}$in (1.25cm) seam allowance. Starting at one edge, stitch 1in (2.5cm), leave $\frac{1}{2}$in (1.25cm) gap for the drawstring, stitch remainder of seam to within 1$\frac{1}{2}$in (4cm) of the end; leave $\frac{1}{2}$in (1.25cm) gap and then stitch to the end. Repeat across the bottom edge.

**3** Turn through to the right side, press and slipstitch the opening. To form the casing, top-stitch $\frac{1}{2}$in (1.25cm) from the top edge. Repeat across the bottom edge.

**4** Cut the pocket piece 26 × 17$\frac{1}{2}$in (66 × 44cm). As with the back piece fold the fabric in half, short ends together. Stitch seam leaving a turning gap in the middle. Refold so that the seam is in the centre and stitch top and bottom seams. Turn through to the right side, press and slipstitch the opening.

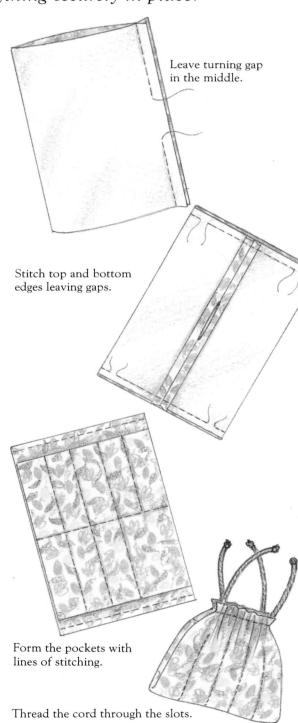

Leave turning gap in the middle.

Stitch top and bottom edges leaving gaps.

Form the pockets with lines of stitching.

Thread the cord through the slots.

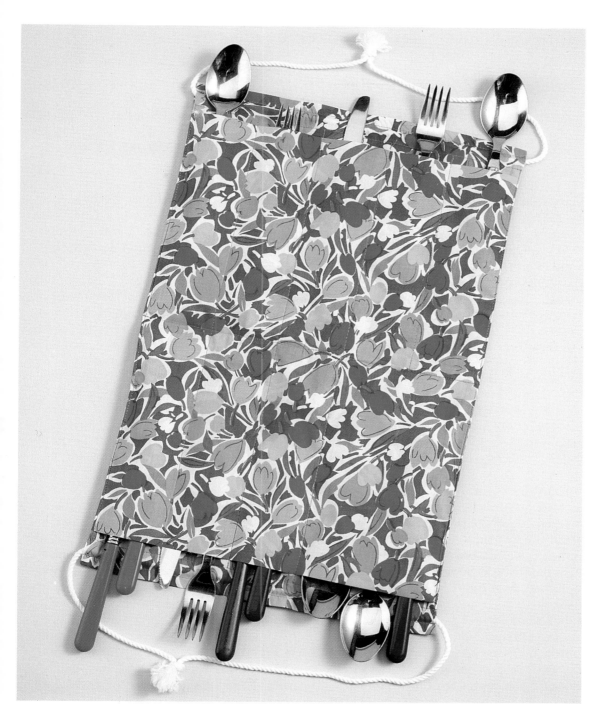

**5** Pin the pocket to the back piece so that it is equal distance from the top and bottom edges. Stitch in place down the side edges and then horizontally across the centre. Form five pockets in the top half, each approx 2½in (6cm) wide for knives, forks, spoons and condiments. Then stitch three more pockets of 2½in (6cm) wide in the bottom half, leaving one end pocket 5in (12cm) wide for the napkins.

**6** Cut the cord in half and thread one each through top and bottom slots, knotting each end. Fold the caddy up and draw the cord together to hold everything securely in place.

# Drawstring beach bag

*Bright and lightweight, this appliquéd beach bag will comfortably carry the necessary paraphernalia for a beach trip and the handy side pockets are ideal for sunglasses and tanning lotion.*

## Materials
½yd (50cm) of 45in (115cm) wide printed cotton
Heavyweight interfacing
Bondaweb remnant
2¼yd (2m) cord
D-ring
Cotton remnants for appliqué motif

## Preparation
1 Cut the bag pieces from the cotton fabric as follows: main bag, 1 piece 12½ × 22in (32 × 56cm); pocket, 1 piece 12½ × 8in (32 × 21cm); cord carrier, 2½ × 3in (6 × 8cm); also cut one 9in (23cm) diameter circle in heavyweight interfacing and two in printed cotton.

2 Hem the top edge of the pocket, turning under ½in (1cm) twice to encase the raw edges. With right sides together, stitch the bottom of the pocket to one end of the main bag section. Then on the right side, stitch pocket sections from top hem to base at 6in (15cm) intervals.

3 Using the graph, scale up the picture of the windsurfer and cut pieces from cotton fabric remnants. Bond the board and each colour panel of the sail and place on the centre front of main bag section, overlapping the panels slightly. Satin stitch around all edges to secure in place before adding the satin stitch boom.

4 Stitch the back seam of the bag, with right sides together, leaving a 1in (2.5cm) opening, 3in (8cm) from the top. Press seam allowance open and neaten both edges.

5 Hem the top edge of the bag by folding over 2½in (6cm) and stitching 1in (2.5cm) from this fold. Turn the raw edge under ½in (1.25cm) and stitch again, catching the raw edge, to form the cord casing.

6 Fold the cord carrier piece in half lengthways, stitch sides together, turn through and press. Thread through the D-ring and then pin the carrier to the base of the bag over the back seam, matching the raw edges.

7 Trim the seam allowance from the circle of interfacing and then sandwich between the two fabric base circles. Turn the bag inside-out and pin to the bases with the cord carrier in place. Machine-stitch and neaten the seam allowance before turning bag through to the right side.

8 Finally thread the cord through the casing at the top of the bag and the D-ring at the base, knotting the ends together firmly.

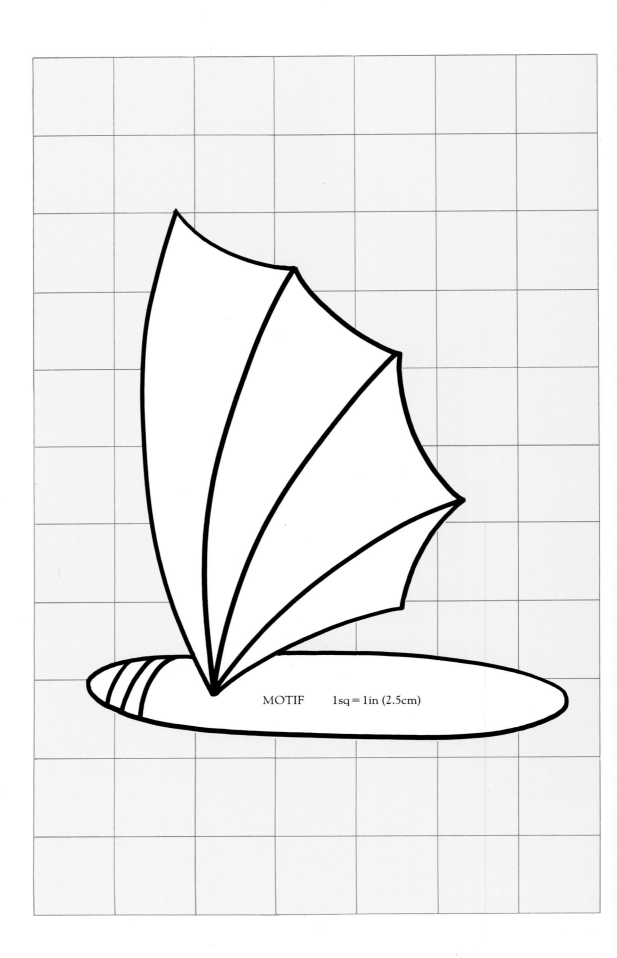

MOTIF 1sq = 1in (2.5cm)

# Creative wall hanging

*Enjoy hours of pleasure making this decorative wall hanging. Let your imagination run wild and fill the shelves with ornaments and books made from fabric remnants.*

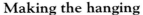

## Materials

Background: 2yd (1.90m) of 36in (90cm)
   wide medium weight fabric
Wallpaper: 22in (56cm) square of printed
   cotton
Ornaments: fabric remnants
Shelves: 4⅜yd (4m) of ½in (1cm) wide
   brown grosgrain ribbon
1yd (90cm) of ½in (1cm) wide white
   grosgrain ribbon
Fans: ¾yd (70cm) each of two shades of
   ¼in (5mm) wide ribbon
Bondaweb and interfacing

## Making the hanging

1 Cut two pieces of the blue background
each 30 × 37in (76 × 94cm). Interface both
front and back background pieces. From
the remaining blue fabric cut three
hangers, each 5 × 10in (13 × 25cm). Cut
the triangle of printed cotton, with two
equal sides 22in (56cm) long, for the
wallpaper.

Pattern for doll motif.

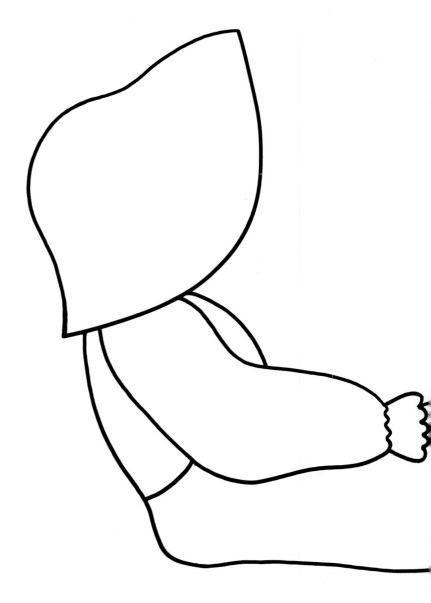

**2** Fold the hangers in half lengthways and sew side seam. Refold so that the seam is in the centre and press. Loop the hangers and pin evenly spaced to the right side, top edge of the back background, matching raw edges.

**3** Place the wallpaper fabric on to the right side of the front background, pinning in place at the top side edges. Cut 5 stair triangles from a plain fabric remnant, each with two equal sides of 4in (10cm). Bond the stairs to the wallpaper, with the long edge of each stair on the inner edge of the wallpaper triangle. Zigzag stitch the stairs in place.

**4** Next add the grosgrain ribbon shelving, with the top shelf placed 2in (5cm) from the top edge, the next four shelves at 5½in (14cm) intervals and the bottom shelf 7in (18cm) lower – approximately 3½in (9cm) from the bottom edge. Finish the shelving with two shelf dividers, one placed 11in (28cm) from the left side on the bottom shelf and the other 18in (46cm) from the left on the next shelf. Add the white grosgrain ribbon to cover the raw edges of the stairs.

**5** Cut out the ornaments from fabric remnants. To make the doll, use the pattern provided; for the other ornaments use household objects as templates such as tea plates for the tea pots, bowl of flowers and fans – drawing the whole plate or part of it as appropriate. Cut different size rectangles for the books using a mix of ribbon and fabric remnants. Weave a wicker basket from the ribbon (see General Techniques) and cut flowers from floral fabric.

**6** Appliqué the ornaments to the wall hanging using Bondaweb and satin stitch. Pad out one or two eggs and the flower bowl to add dimension. Trim the large eggs with decorative ribbon and add titles to some books. Make the fan spines from strips of narrow ribbon topped by lace trim. Add a hand embroidered flower to the top bowl and a little bow to the doll's shoe.

**7** Once the decoration is complete, pin the front to the back, with right sides together, sandwiching the hangers. Machine-stitch around the outer edge, leaving a turning gap in the bottom edge. Turn through and press. Slipstitch the opening.

**8** To make the lower pole casing fold the bottom end up 1½in (4cm). Machine-stitch close to the edge.

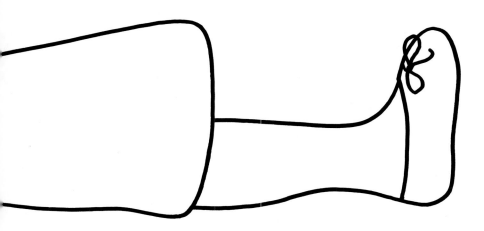

# Tidy travel sewing caddy

*Designed with travelling in mind, this petite sewing caddy is practical and pretty. Individual pockets hold the chosen haberdashery that will ensure you are prepared for any emergency.*

## Materials
Fabric remnant approx 11 × 36in
   (28 × 90cm)
Interfacing remnant approx 11 × 7in
   (28 × 18cm)
1yd (90cm) of 1in (2.5cm) wide satin bias
   binding
20in (51cm) of ¼in (6mm) wide ribbon for
   ties

## Making the caddy
**1** Cut the back, lining, pocket and needle threader strap from the main fabric as follows: back and lining each 11 × 6½in (28 × 17cm); pocket 11in (28cm) square; strap 2½ × 2in (6.5 × 5cm). Cut the interfacing to the same size as the back.

**2** Attach the interfacing to the wrong side of the back piece, then quilt for a decorative finish. (Use a ready-printed interfacing with quilting guidelines for quick and easy quilting.)

**3** Fold the strap section in half lengthways right sides together, and machine-stitch the long edge. Turn through and fold both ends under ¼in (6mm), press in place.

**4** Fold the pocket section in half to measure 11 × 5½in (28 × 14cm) and then pin it to the lining section, matching side edges and raw edges at the bottom edge.

**5** Machine-stitch the five individual pockets by stitching from top to bottom – the first line of stitching 3in (8cm) from the left edge and the remaining three, 2in (5cm) apart. Then pin the strap to the centre front of the second pocket, stitching in place at either side.

**6** Pin the pocket and lining to the quilted back with wrong sides together and then round-off the corners, cutting through all layers. Fold the ribbon tie in half and with the quilted side of the backing uppermost, pin the folded edge to the right hand side seam allowance approximately 3½in (9cm) from the top corner.

**7** Open out the satin binding and pin around the edges of the sewing caddy working from the quilted side. Stitch through all layers. Fold the binding over to the pocket side, encasing the raw edges, and slipstitch in place. Then fold down the top edge of the caddy to cover the pocket openings. Press with a damp cloth to give a good permanent crease.

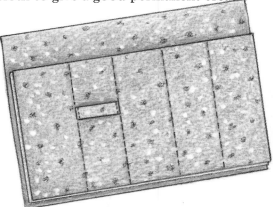

Machine stitch the five pockets.

**8** Fill the pockets with haberdashery, slipping embroidery scissors in the wider end pocket, with buttons, needles, and pins in the remaining pockets. Make a thread carrier from a piece of card $1\frac{1}{2} \times 5$in ($4 \times 13$cm). Snip grooves down one side and wind on lengths of thread, securing the ends through the snipped grooves.

# Perfectly pleated lampshade

*Add the finishing touches to your room décor with this cleverly pleated coolie shade. To give a soft warm glow for romantic evenings, just add a pastel-coloured lining.*

**Materials**

Main fabric: for the cover, measure a strut to determine the height of the shade and add 2in (5cm). Measure the circumference of the lower ring and multiply it by two to determine the total length of fabric required
2¼yd (2.10m) tape binding
½yd (50cm) lining
1yd (90cm) bias binding

**Making the lampshade**

**1** First bind the frame by wrapping the tape tightly and evenly around the struts, top and bottom rings. Stitch the ends in place to prevent unravelling. This will then provide a surface on which to stitch the lining.

**2** Line the inside of the frame by first cutting two rectangles of lining slightly larger than half-frame size. Lay each piece over the frame, pull taut and pin in place, pinning the two pieces together at the sides. Keeping the pins in the lining, carefully remove from the frame. Trim off excess fabric, leaving ½in (1.25cm) seam allowance at either side and approximately 1in (2.5cm) at top and bottom.

**3** Machine-stitch the side seams and then neaten the top and bottom edges by turning under ½in (1.25cm). Fit the lining to the inside of the frame so that the seams are over the struts and the seam allowances face outwards. Pin around the top and bottom, stretching the fabric taut. Hand sew in place.

**4** For the cover, cut the fabric to size – the height plus 1in (2.5cm) and the circumference doubled. Join pieces end to end if necessary to get the total length required. Turn the top and bottom edges under ½in (1.25cm) twice to neaten.

**5** Pin one side edge of the cover to the top and bottom of one strut with ½in (1.25cm) overlapping top and bottom. Make tight pleats around the top of the shade, pinning each pleat through the top ring. Adjust the fullness as you go, finishing with the final pleat overlapping the first one.

**6** Pin the lower end of the pleats to the bottom ring, again adjusting the fullness as you go. Once the pleats are pinned in place, oversew the cover to the frame, holding the fabric taut and removing the pins as you go. Trim the excess fabric away, close to the stitching at the top and bottom.

**7** Hand sew the bias binding around the top and bottom of the lampshade, right sides facing, to cover the fabric edges. Fold the binding to the inside and catch stitch in place.

---

**Sewing tip**

When you have pinned the 2 pieces of lining fabric together at the sides of the frame (right sides facing), run a soft pencil or dressmaker's chalk pencil down the side struts, marking the fabric, before you take the lining off the frame. This will give you a guideline for stitching the side seams, and getting a perfect fit.

**Quick-make shades**

**Pretty and lacy** Make a cover for a plain, white lampshade using broderie anglaise fabric. Measure round the bottom of the lampshade. Cut fabric to three times the measurement by the depth of the shade plus 1in (2.5cm). Join the short ends. Press a $\frac{1}{2}$in (1.25cm) to the right side on top and bottom edges. Stitch broderie anglaise edging round the bottom edge. Gather the top edge to fit the lampshade top ring. Thread ribbon through 1$\frac{1}{2}$in (4cm)-wide broderie anglaise eyelet edging. Sew the edging round the top of the cover. Then sew a ribbon bow with streamer ends at the front of the shade.

**Mock pleating** Bind the struts and rings of a drum-shaped shade. Catch the end of 1in (2.5cm)-wide taffeta feather-edged ribbon to the inside of the bottom ring. Bind the ribbon over the frame, overlapping the edges a little. Finish the ribbon end at the bottom ring, turning it under and catching it to the inside of the ring.

# Sewing basket

*Customizing a plain basket into an attractive sewing accessory makes a great gift idea. The lining has side pockets to hold threads and tapes, whilst a pin cushion and lid add the finishing touches.*

## Materials

12in (30cm) diameter basket requires:
⅞yd (80cm) of 36in (90cm) wide fabric
½ yard (50cm) of 36in (90cm) wide plain fabric
12 × 24in (31.5 × 61cm) of 4oz (100g) wadding
1yd (90cm) of narrow ribbon or elastic
2yd (1.90m) of 1½in (4cm) wide ribbon
1yd (90cm) of ¼in (5mm) elastic for pocket tops
Fabric-covered button
Felt scraps

## Making the basket

**1** To calculate the fabric required for any basket first measure around the outside, adding an extra 1½in (4cm) for ease and seam allowance. Then measure the height from base to rim, adding an extra 3in (8cm) for overlap, casing and seam allowances.

**2** Cut the fabric to the required measurement for the lining. For the pockets cut another strip the same length × basket height plus 1in (2.5cm) seam allowance. Next cut the frill 3in (8cm) wide × the length and a half (joining strips if necessary to get the total length). From the plain fabric, cut 1 base section which should measure the actual size plus 1in (2.5cm) seam allowance. Cut 1 base from the wadding.

**3** To make the pockets turn one long edge of the pocket piece under ¾in (2cm) turning the raw edge under again and stitch close to the turned edge to form an elastic casing. Before inserting elastic divide the total length into six equal sections for the pockets and press in creases. Then insert the ¼in (6mm) elastic, and pull up slightly. Pin the wrong side of the pocket piece to the right side of the lining, matching bottom edges. Machine-stitch together along the crease lines to form the pockets. Then stitch the short ends of both strips together to form a ring.

**4** With right sides together, pin the lining pockets to the circular base, encasing and gathering the sides to fit evenly as you go. Add the wadding to the underside of the base and machine-stitch through all thickness. Cut two 'V' shapes in the top edge of the lining to go round the handles. Bind the raw edges with binding made from bias strips of the main fabric.

**5** Cut the frill into two lengths and then fold each in half lengthways with wrong sides together. Gather the long edges and then pin and stitch to the right side of the lining 1½in (4cm) from the top edge. Turn the top edge over towards the frill to form hem and casing, tucking raw edges under ½in (1.25cm) and encasing the raw edges of the frill at the same time.

**6** Place the finished lining in the basket, with sides and frill folded over the rim. Insert the narrow ribbon or elastic through the slot under the frill to hold the lining in place.

**7** To make the lid base, cut a lid-sized circle each in plain fabric, interfacing and wadding and pin together in that order. For the gathered lid cover, measure around the outer edge adding 1in (2.5cm) seam allowance multiplied by the radius

plus ½in (1.25cm). Cut a strip of main fabric to this length and stitch end to end to form a ring. Fold over ½in (1.25cm) on one edge and gather using large stitches. Pull up tightly and fasten off.

8 Pin the remaining raw edge, right side uppermost to the outer edge of the 3-layer lid base with the plain fabric on the bottom. Stitch ¼in (6mm) from the edge to hold the layers together. Neaten the edges with binding, made from strips of plain fabric cut on the bias and joined end to end. Finish the lid with a covered button in the centre. Tie a ribbon bow to each handle to decorate the basket.

9 For the pin cushion, cut a saucer-size circle of plain fabric for the centre. Gather around the outer edges, pull up and stuff firmly with spare wadding. Cut a strip of patterned fabric 16 × 3½in (41 × 9cm). Stitch end to end to form a ring and fold in half lengthways wrong sides together. Turn raw edges to inside and press. Using large stitches gather edges and pull up tightly, fasten off. Stitch padded centre in place and add felt leaves.

# Holiday tablecloth

*A festive Christmas table starts with the cloth and this parcel design has plenty of surprises in store with the elasticated pockets which make super hidey-holes for little gifts.*

## Materials

To fit 57 × 35in (145 × 89cm) table

2yd (1.90m) of red sheeting 90in (228cm) wide

1¾yd (1.50m) of 36in (90cm) wide green printed cotton

3½yd (3.20m) of 3in (8cm) wide satin ribbon

1⅜yd (1.20m) of ⅛in (3mm) wide elastic

## Making the tablecloth

**1** Hem around the red sheeting, turning raw edge under ¼in (6mm) twice and machine-stitching. Mitre each corner.

**2** Using the green printed cotton, cut 2 parcel strips 44 × 10in (112 × 25cm) and stitch together to form one long strip of 88in (224cm). Cut a further 2 strips

33 × 10in (84 × 25cm) and again, stitch them together to form one long strip 66in (168cm).

**3** Neaten the sides of each strip by turning raw edge under ½in (1.25cm). Turn each end under twice, to completely encase the raw edges. Machine-stitch across the end and approx 4¼in (11cm) up each side. Then gather-stitch across each end of both strips approx 4in (10cm) from the hem, and pull up so that the gathered material is 5½in (14cm) wide.

**4** Position the parcel ties on the red cloth, crossing them at the centre. Machine-stitch down the side edges of both strips stopping at the gathered-stitching and thus leaving the remaining

ends free. Cut the ribbon into 4 equal lengths, tie each one into a bow and add a large red bow at the gathered end of each parcel strip.

**5** To make the surprise pockets fold the patterned fabric in half lengthways and cut 8 pocket shapes using the pattern. Hem the top edge and then turn under and press ½in (1.25cm) on the remaining edges. Cut a 6in (15cm) length of elastic for each pocket and stitch to the wrong side of the pocket, 1in (2.5cm) from the top hem, stretching the elastic to full width as you go.

**6** Finally top stitch a pocket either side of the parcel strips, placing them level with the ribbon bows.

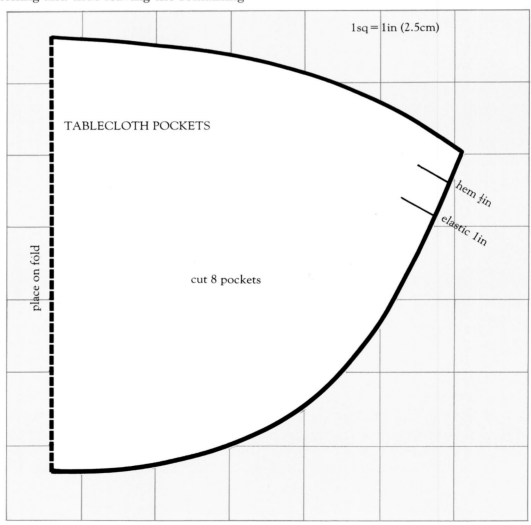

1sq = 1in (2.5cm)

TABLECLOTH POCKETS

place on fold

cut 8 pockets

hem ½in

elastic 1in

# Santa Claus stocking

Hang this colourful Christmas stocking above the mantelpiece ready for Santa Claus to fill it with lots of surprises. The full boot shape ensures plenty of room to pack in presents.

## Materials

To make 2 stockings:
20in (51cm) of 36in (90cm) wide red felt
White and green felt squares
Black fabric paint
Oddment of orange felt
DK wool oddments and polyester
   stuffing
1yd (90cm) of 1in (2.5cm) wide satin ribbon
Decorative fluffy balls and sequins

## Making the stockings

**1** Fold the ends of the felt to meet in the middle and using the graph pattern cut 2 stocking pieces for each stocking. For the snowman, fold a square of white felt in half and placing the pattern against the fold, cut one body and head piece. Cut holly from green felt.

**2** Using the fabric paint, paint the coal black eyes and mouth on the face and leaf detail on the holly. Alternatively, embroider French knot eyes and use a running stitch for the mouth. Next, cut a triangle of orange felt for the carrot nose. Fold in half and stitch two sides together, lightly stuff and hand sew to the centre of the face.

**3** Whilst the paint dries, knit the woolly hat and scarf. For the hat, cast on 10 stitches of DK yarn. Knit two rows, working in stocking stitch (stockinet stitch). Decrease at each end of the next and alternate rows until one stitch remains. Cast off. For the scarf, cast on 4 stitches and garter-stitch for 10 rows. Change colour if desired and knit another 10 rows. Change to a third colour for the next 20 rows, then repeat colours one and two for another 10 rows each. Add a ½in (1.25cm) fringe to each end.

**4** Wrap the scarf around the snowman's neck and then pin him to one boot section approximately in the centre. Machine-stitch around the edges, stopping either side of the scarf and leaving an opening at the top. Stuff lightly, pushing the stuffing through the neck and rounding out his tummy. Slipstitch the opening and then hand sew the woolly hat at a jaunty angle.

**5** Finish the snowman with a pompon for his hat and fluffy balls for his tummy held firmly in place by adhesive fabric paint/glue. Add a group of white fluffy snowballs, attached with fabric paint.

**6** Position the holly leaves as desired on the boot and hand sew in place. Add groups of red sequin berries.

**7** Fold the top of both boot sections under 1in (2.5cm) and stitch in place. Cut a 9in (23cm) length of satin ribbon for the hanging loop. Then pin the back to the front boot section with wrong sides together, pinning the ribbon loop in the seam allowance at the top edge. Using a contrasting coloured thread, machine-stitch around the boot edges, allowing ½in (1.25cm) seam allowance. Trim to ¼in (6mm) from the stitching.

**8** Tie the remaining ribbon into a decorative bow for the top of the boot. Catch stitch in place at the centre front.

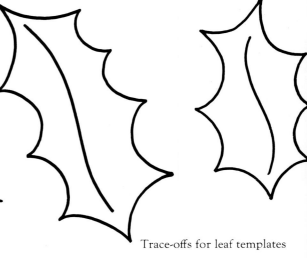

Trace-offs for leaf templates

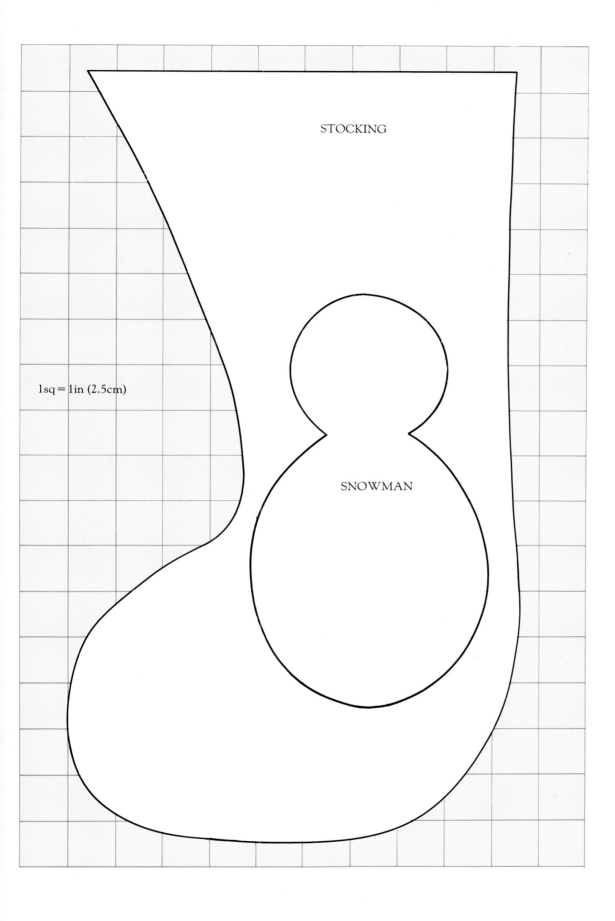

STOCKING

1sq = 1in (2.5cm)

SNOWMAN

# Christmas tree skirt

*Finish the tree decorations with these festive frills. A pretty, but practical tree skirt will hide unsightly pots or stands and provide a perfect backdrop for your pile of presents.*

### Materials
1yd (90cm) of 36in (90cm) printed cotton
½yd (50cm) of red cotton fabric
15½in (38.5cm) Velcro

### Making the skirt
1  To cut the circle for the tree skirt, first fold the main fabric in quarters to form a square of four layers. Pin one end of a length of thread 17½in (45cm) long to the folded corner. Pivoting from this point mark off the radius of the skirt. Cut along this curved line through all layers.

2  With the fabric still folded in four, measure 1½in (4cm) from the folded corner down either side. Draw a line between the marked points. Cut along this line through all layers to make the top hole.

3  Open out circle of fabric and cut skirt from outside edge to centre hole along one of the creases. Narrow hem the centre hole, turning the edge under ¼in (6mm) twice to encase the raw edge. Turn the side edges under ½in (1.25cm) and press. Then pin strips of Velcro down both side edges and machine-stitch in place.

4  Cut the red cotton into 2½in (6cm) wide strips and then sew them end to end to form one long strip. Fold this in half lengthways with wrong sides together, and gather-stitch along the raw edges. Pull up so that the frill is approximately half its original length.

5  With right sides together, pin the gathered frill to the outside edge of the skirt. Adjust gathers as necessary and machine-stitch. Press the seam allowance towards the skirt and then edge-stitch to the skirt base.

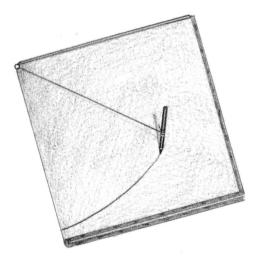

Fold the fabric into four
and mark off the radius of the skirt.

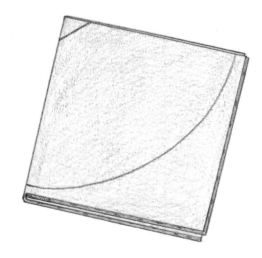

Draw a line across the folded corner.

# Advent calendar

*Countdown to Christmas with this easy-to-make advent calendar. A mixture of sweets and little gifts tied to the numbered rings ensures a special little surprise every day.*

## Materials
17 × 24½in (43 × 62cm) red felt
12½ × 28½in (32 × 72cm) green felt
Brown felt square
Gold fabric paint
1½yd (1.40m) of ⅛in (3mm) wide ribbon
   for ties
24 brass curtain rings
1yd (1m) wide satin ribbon
20in (51cm) dowel ½in (1.25cm) diameter

## Making the calendar
1 Take the red felt background and turn one end and both sides under ¾in (2cm) then top-stitch ½in (1.25cm) from the edge. Turn the remaining (top) edge under 1½in (4cm) and machine-stitch 1in (2.5cm) from edge to form casing for the dowel.

2 From the green felt cut 3 tree shapes as shown in the pattern. The first has a 12½in (32cm) base. The middle shape has an 11in (28cm) base whilst the top triangle has an 8½in (22cm) base with two equal sides 6½in (16cm).

3 Place the largest tree piece on the background 2½in (6cm) from the bottom edge. Then add the middle and top triangle overlapping each other so that the top of the tree is 2in (5cm) below the top edge of the background.

4 Before bonding and stitching in place, carefully stencil the numbers 1–24 in gold paint randomly scattered on all three tree sections. Then attach the tree shapes to

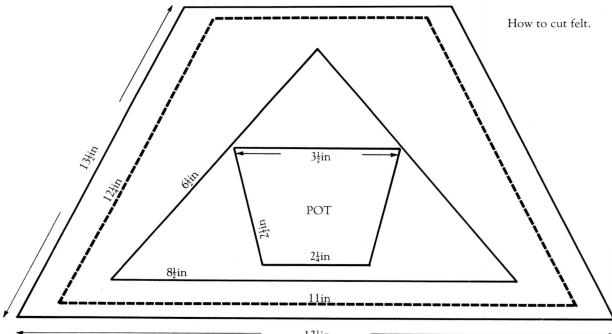

How to cut felt.

the background with Bondaweb and a large machine-stitch around the outer edges to secure.

**5** Cut out and add the brown felt tree pot. Bond in place and then machine-stitch to secure.

**6** Hand sew a brass curtain ring below each date from which to hang the daily surprises. It is now ready to add the

individually wrapped gifts, tied in place with ribbon bows.

**7** To hang the calendar, cut the wide ribbon into two halves, fold and stitch one end of each to form a loop. Insert the dowel through the top casing, adding a ribbon loop to either end. Then tie the remaining ribbon ends into a decorative bow.

## PART THREE

# For Babies and Children

# Introduction to Part Three

*There are few occupations more rewarding than making things for small children. Whether you sew, embroider, do woodwork or paint, there is something here for you.*

Sooner or later, most parents realise that children need surroundings, toys and equipment all of their own. If you can provide some of these by making them yourself, you will save a great deal of money, as well as having the satisfaction of having created something different for your child and for your friends' children.

Many parents today feel that they have no time for crafts. The problems of establishing a secure home and providing one's children with the upbringing that will equip them for life in the 21st century, take priority. This is understandable. It is quicker to dash into the local shop and buy coverlets, wall hangings, counting panels, pictures and other accessories. The things you can buy are good quality and well-made and we

should not deprecate them. But, until you have made something yourself, you are missing one of the most satisfying feelings in the world.

Children react in a most reassuring way to something you have made for them. If your expertise is not all you might want it to be, children are far from critical. You made it especially for them. That is what matters most. Fathers come into their own with hand-made toys. Even if a man feels that he is the most thumb-fingered of individuals when it comes to handling wood, the pleasure of seeing the wide-eyed wonder of a child given something that Daddy made himself, is not to be missed.

The arrival of a new baby is a good opportunity for giving presents and hand-

made gifts are always greatly appreciated on these occasions. Mothers rarely have enough time, before or after the birth, to make quilts and other nursery furnishings, so this is where relatives – and friends – come in. If you are a grandmother, mother, aunt, sister, cousin or an affectionate friend, you will find lots of things here that make marvellous gifts. Whatever your interest: decorative sewing, embroidery, painting, stencilling or toymaking, there is something here for you.

Some of the projects are quick to do and can be completed in a few hours. Others take more time. But they are all very simple to make, using only basic techniques. The rag book is really fun to do and you will have a lot of pleasure in making this. Bright and colourful, with some amusing ideas in it, the rag book provides practice for small hands in tying bows, fastening zippers and press fasteners and coping with buttons and buttonholes – important skills when a child begins to dress himself. There is a play mat here too, very fishy with a sea, seashore, sunfish rattles and a starfish hand puppet.

For the older children, a farmyard scene, complete with animals, birds and farm folk, will provide hours of amusement – and they will learn to count at the same time.

For woodwork enthusiasts, the rocking hen toy will make a very special gift and provides a lasting source of fun for children as they grow. The push-along pigeon will entertain babies when they are learning to walk, as well as toddlers.

The pretty baby slippers are easy enough for beginners to make and the cross stitch picture of ducks is something even older children could attempt.

Whichever project you choose to start with, you can be sure you will want to go back and make more!

# Patchwork ball

*This fascinating play ball is made from fabric segments stuffed and sewn together. Babies love these balls because they are so easy for little hands to hold.*

**Materials**
Tracing paper
8 × 45in (20 × 115cm) piece of plain fabric
(inner sections)
6 × 45in (15 × 115cm) piece of patterned
fabric (outer sections)
Washable polyester toy filling
Strong buttonhole thread

**Preparation**
1  Trace the pattern for the outer section.
Draw and cut out a paper circle 7¼in
(18.5cm) diameter. Cut the circle in half
for the inner section pattern. (A ¼in
(6mm) seam allowance is included on the
patterns.) Cut 12 inner sections from
plain fabric and 12 outer sections from
patterned fabric.

**Working the design**
2  With right sides facing, fold an inner
section in half. Stitch along the straight
edges about half way.

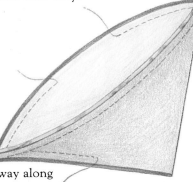

Stitch halfway along
the straight edges.

3  Pin and baste the edges of the outer
section to the inner section. Starting in
the middle of a side, machine-stitch all
round. Turn to the right side and stuff
the segment firmly. Oversew to close the
opening. Repeat with all the segments.

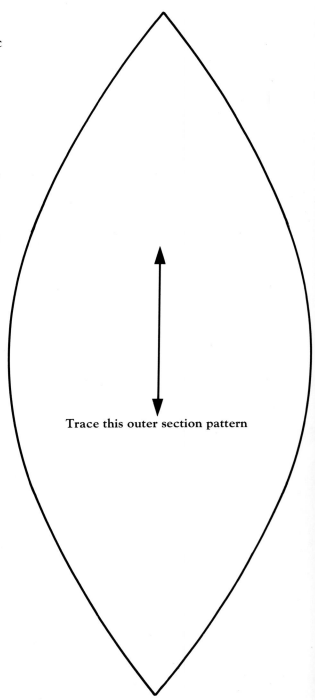

**Trace this outer section pattern**

## Finishing

**4** Take 2 segments and, using buttonhole thread, join them with a ⅜in (9mm) buttonhole bar (A-B). Join 2 more (C-D) in the same way, between A and B, but this time interweave the two buttonhole bars at the centre.

**5** Join the outer points of the segments in the same way with buttonhole bars. Join four more segments to the first four, placing them at right angles. Interweave the buttonhole bars at the centre and outer points. Join in the four remaining segments.

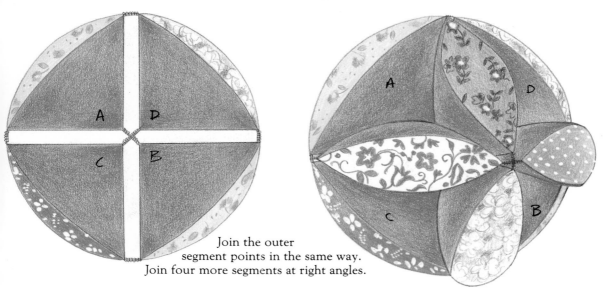

Join the outer
segment points in the same way.
Join four more segments at right angles.

117

# Rag book

*Small children are fascinated by colourful rag books which help them to learn about buttons and button holes, press fasteners, zip fasteners and simple ties.*

## Materials

Squared pattern paper
Light-weight iron-on interfacing
Pieces of plain fabric in jade, green, yellow and blue, each 11 × 18in (28 × 45cm)
Scraps of brightly coloured, plain and patterned fabrics
Pieces of coloured felt
Trimmings: ricrac braid, ribbons, lace etc
Stranded embroidery cottons
Washable polyester toy filling
12in (30cm) strip of touch-and-hold fastening

Fabric writing pens
Narrow green satin ribbon
Red ribbon
3 large buttons
12 large press fasteners
Small strip of thin cardboard
Light-weight green zip fastener, 7in (18cm) long
Sew-in, medium weight interfacing, 33 × 36in (88 × 90cm)
Sew-in, heavyweight interfacing, 8½ × 18in (21 × 45cm)
Large button (for cover tab)

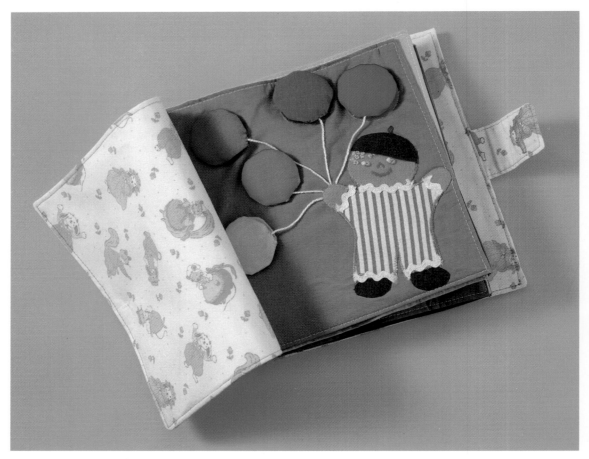

## Preparation

**1** Draw the pattern pieces on squared paper, working on the fold where indicated on the pattern piece. Identify the various segments as indicated on the patterns. Cut out.

**2** Iron light-weight interfacing onto the wrong side of any fabrics which might fray. Spread the fabric pieces for pairs of pages 1 and 8 (jade), 2 and 7 (green), 3 and 6 (yellow) and 4 and 5 (blue). Measure and mark the page area on each piece, 9in (23cm) deep by 16½in (43cm) wide, using chalk. This includes a ¼in (6mm) turning all round.

## Working the design

**3** PAGE 1 BALLOON SELLER: Spread the jade fabric for pages 1 and 8. Page 1 is on the right-hand side. Using the balloon seller pattern, cut the entire shape in striped fabric then the head and hands from pink felt, and the boots and beret from blue felt.

**4** Machine-applique the balloon seller to the right-hand corner, about ½in (1cm) inside the chalked outline. Sew on the felt face, hands and boots and beret. Embroider the features, trim with ricrac braid.

**5** Cut five 1½in (4cm)-diameter circles

from different coloured fabrics for balloon bases. Machine-appliqué the circles to the background fabric (refer to the picture for positions).

**6** Cut 2 circles, each 2⅜in (6cm) diameter, from the same colour fabrics, for the balloons. Make up the balloons, using the detached appliqué technique. Sew the ball part of the press fasteners to the balloon bases and the other part to the backs of the balloons. Fix the balloons in place then attach a length of coloured thread to each balloon with the other end fixed to the hand. Write 'Match my colours' on the background, using a fabric pen.

**7** OPPOSITE PAGE (8) Cut 2 flower shapes from each of three fabrics, yellow, red and orange. Cut 4 green leaves. From flowered fabric, cut a window box 1¼ × 6¼in (3 × 16cm).

**8** Machine-appliqué the window box near to the bottom edge of the page. Appliqué a 3½in (9cm) piece of narrow green ribbon up from the middle for the flower stem and attach a leaf on each side, at an angle (refer to the picture). Appliqué the remaining two leaves across the corners of the window box.

**9** Place pairs of flowers together, wrong

Scale: 1 sq = 1in (2.5cm)

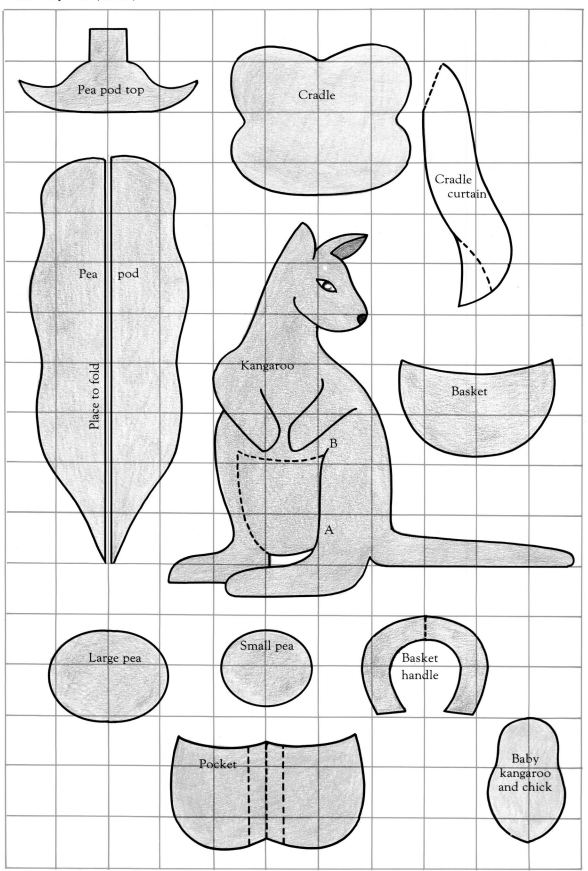

Pea pod top

Cradle

Cradle curtain

Pea    pod

Place to fold

Kangaroo

B

A

Basket

Large pea

Small pea

Basket handle

Pocket

Baby kangaroo and chick

Flower

Leaf

Balloon seller

Lower
tree trunk

Upper
tree trunk

Eggshell

Cat

Ladybird

Tree foliage

sides facing, and work machine satin stitch round the edges. Work a buttonhole in each flower. Sew buttons onto the page. Button on the flowers. Write 'Button the flowers' in fabric pen.

**10** PAGES 2 AND 7 (GREEN): The cat design is on the left-hand side. Using the pattern, cut the cat body from orange fabric, then the stripes, stomach and features from cream fabric. Baste the middle of a 20in (50cm) length of red ribbon under the cat's neck. Appliqué the details to the cat and the cat to the background. Embroider the eyes in detached chain stitch, the mouth in running stitch and the whiskers in straight stitch. Write 'Tie the bow'.

**11** PAGE 7: (Right-hand page.) Cut the ladybird body in red fabric and the head in black fabric. Cut the spots from black felt. Appliqué the ladybird to the background fabric, then add the head and spots. Embroider the legs in chain stitch and running stitch and the feelers in straight stitch. Work the eyes and wing line in running stitch. Write 'Count the spots' in fabric pen.

**12** PAGES 3 AND 6: Work page 3 (apple tree) on the right-hand side of the fabric piece. Cut 2 upper tree trunks and 1

lower trunk. Cut 1 basket handle. Cut 12 red felt apples each ⅓in (2cm) in diameter. Cut 2 baskets and 2 tree tops. Cut 1 yellow fabric pocket (to hold the lower tree trunk) 2½ × 7in (6 × 18cm).

**13** BASKET: Machine-appliqué the basket handle to the lower right hand corner of the page. Stitch 2 basket pieces together, right sides facing, leaving a gap for turning. Turn to the right side. Oversew to close the seam. Machine-stitch the basket to the background, below the basket handle, so that the basket forms a pouch.

**14** TREE: The upper trunk pulls up out of the pocket. Stitch the upper tree trunks to the foliage, underlapping the trunks. With wrong sides facing, place the foliage pieces together and work narrow machine satin stitch round the edges, leaving a gap. Stuff the foliage lightly and continue stitching to close the gap. Cut a piece of cardboard ¾ × 6in (2 × 15cm) and slide it up into the tree trunk to stiffen it. Stitch the bottom edge of the tree trunk.

**15** POCKET: Appliqué the lower tree trunk centrally to one end of the pocket piece (about ¼in (6mm) from the short end). Right sides facing, fold the pocket

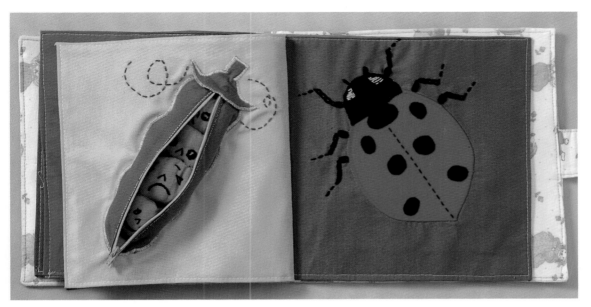

in half widthways and stitch to within ¼in (6mm) of the edges, leaving a gap for turning. Turn to the right side. Top-stitch the pocket to the page beside the basket, leaving the upper edge open. Slip the stiffened tree trunk inside the pocket. Catch the bottom corners of the trunk inside the pocket with sufficient length of thread to enable it to be pulled up.

**16** APPLES: Oversew the felt apples together in pairs. Sew the ball part of the press fasteners to the foliage and the other half to the apples. Sew narrow ribbons to the apples and fasten the ribbon ends inside the basket. Embroider flowers and leaves under the tree and basket. Write 'Pick the apples' on the page using fabric pen.

**17** PAGE 6: This is on the left-hand side of the yellow pages 3 and 6. Cut 1 pea pod top. Cut 4 small peas and 4 larger ones, adding ¼in (6mm) all round. Cut 2 pea pod halves from folded fabric, placing the straight edge of the pattern on the fold.

**18** Stitch the zip fastener between the folded edges of the pea pod halves, placing the top of the zipper at the rounded end. Stitch the edges together below the point.

**19** Place two matching pea pieces together, right sides facing and stitch round, leaving a gap. Stuff and close the gap. Embroider faces on the peas.

**20** Pin the peas inside the pod, place the pod on the page and mark round the edges with chalk. Remove the pod and stitch one side of a 6in (15cm) strip of touch-and-hold fastening down the middle of the pod outline. Cut the other side into 4 pieces and sew to the backs of the peas. Work narrow machine satin stitch round the edges of the pea pod to appliqué it to the page. Work satin stitch round the pod top. Pin it in place, appliqué the top to the page. Put the peas in the pod and zip up. Write 'Put the peas in the pod' using fabric pen.

**21** PAGES 4 AND 5 (BLUE): The kangaroo design is on the left and the cradle is on the right. Cut out the entire kangaroo. Adding seam allowance, cut 2 kangaroo pockets and 2 kangaroo babies. Appliqué the kangaroo to the page. Sew a small piece of touch-and-hold fastening to the kangaroo in the pocket position. Embroider the details on the kangaroo chest with straight stitches. Make up the pocket. Machine-appliqué to the kangaroo along A-B. Slipstitch round the curved edge.

123

**22** Make up two kangaroo baby pieces, stuff and embroider the features. Sew on felt ears. Sew the other side of the touch-and-hold strip to the back of the baby. Pop into the pocket.

**23** PAGE 5: Cut 2 cradle curtains, reversing the pattern for one. Adding ⅛in (6mm) seam allowance, cut 2 chicks, 2 eggshells and 2 cradles. Appliqué the cradle curtains to the right-hand side of the page and add a lace motif to top centre (refer to the picture). Sew one side of a small piece of touch-and-hold fastening to the page for the cradle and eggshell positions (refer to the picture). Stitch 2 pieces of cradle together, right sides facing, leaving a gap. Do the same with the eggshell pieces. Work a stem stitch edge to the cradle. Slipstitch the cradle to the page, overlapping the curtain edges. Slipstitch the eggshell to the left of the cradle.

**24** PAGE 5: Make up the chick and stuff it. Embroider the eyes and sew on a felt beak. Sew one side of a piece of touch-and-hold fastening to the back of the chick. Write 'Put the baby to bed' across pages 4 and 5, using a fabric pen.

**Finishing**
**25** Press the work on the wrong side, trim the pages back to the chalked

outlines. Cut medium weight interfacing ⅛in (6mm) smaller all round and baste to the wrong side of the pages. Turn and press the page edges to the wrong side. Pin and baste page 2 and 7 to the back of pages 1 and 8 and top-stitch all round. Top-stitch pages 3 and 6 to pages 4 and 5.

**26** FASTENING TAB: Cut a piece of heavyweight non-woven interfacing 1½ × 2½in (4 × 6cm) and a piece of the cover fabric 1½ × 6in (4 × 15cm). Fold the fabric in half widthways with right sides facing and join the two long edges, taking a ⅛in (6mm) seam. Turn to the right side and insert the interfacing. Work a buttonhole on the folded end of the tab and top-stitch all round the edges, except the open end.

**27** COVER: Cut 2 pieces of fabric each 9¼ × 19in (23.5 × 48cm), and a piece of heavyweight interfacing to the same size. Place the fabric pieces together with right sides facing and pin the interfacing on top. Stitch round through all thicknesses leaving one short side open for turning. Turn to the right side and press in the opening edges ⅛in (6mm). Tuck the raw end of the tab underneath the middle of the edge and baste, then top-stitch. Arrange the pages in order and stitch down the spine. Sew a button on the cover. Finish with a ribbon bow.

# Farmyard counting panel

*This cheerful wall hanging for the nursery is not only decorative and amusing but will help a small child to learn to count. Hang it where it can be reached easily.*

## Materials

Squared pattern paper

24 × 33in (60 × 84cm) piece of pelmet-weight non-woven interfacing

12 × 33in (30 × 84cm) piece of blue fabric (sky, section 9)

Pieces of plain and patterned fabric for the fields, garden, house etc (refer to the picture)

½yd (45cm) each of white and green ricrac braid

Pieces of coloured felt (including beige, white and black)

Stranded embroidery cottons

39in (1m) of ⅞in (2cm)-wide touch-and-hold fastening

Washable polyester toy filling

24 × 33in (60 × 84cm) piece of fabric for backing

39in (1m) of ½in (1cm)-diameter wooden dowelling

45in (115cm) of ·1in (2.5cm)-wide ribbon

### Preparation

**1** Draw the pattern of the farmyard layout on squared paper. Number the sections and cut them apart. Pin each section to its relevant fabric and cut out with ¼in (6mm) seam allowance all round.

**2** Draw the figures, animals and bird patterns on squared paper. Cut out the patterns. Using them, cut the basic shape twice, once from coloured felt (see the patterns for a guide) and once from beige felt. Some of the figures are reversed left to right for variety.

**3** Still using the patterns, cut the appliqué pieces from felt (the children's clothes, the cows' spots, noses and hooves, tree foliage, apples and leaves etc). Baste, then sew in place.

### Make a farmyard game

First, prepare the farmyard layout on a piece of stiff board, using coloured papers instead of fabric. Make the animals and figures in card and paper also. Make a set for each player. On the farmyard layout, stick numbers from **1** to **12**, with the farmhouse position as **12**. Stick numbers on the figures and animals.

To play, two dice are thrown and the player decides which of the figures or animals he will position on the farmyard. He can add the two dice together to make a single number (ie two sixes to make the twelve for the farmhouse) or he can use the individual dice numbers to place two pieces. The winner is the first player to have placed all his pieces, the others counting the pieces left over against their score.

The skill lies in deciding how to use the dice numbers. For instance, a player may have positioned the farmhouse with 12, and then is unable to throw sixes, which is the number for the sheep. He could be left with 3 pieces, instead of just one.

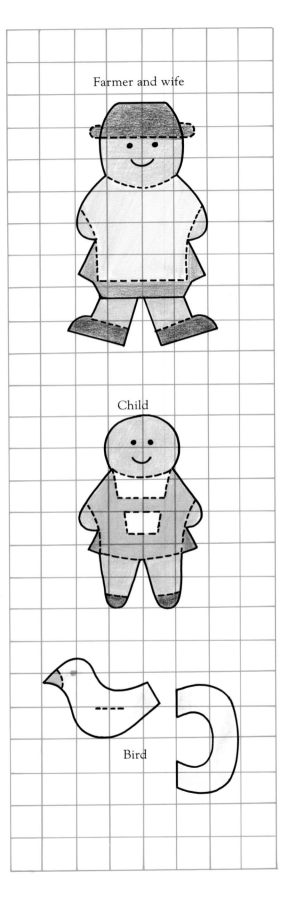

Farmer and wife

Child

Bird

Scale: 1 sq = ½in (1cm)

Farmhouse

Hen

Flower

Cow

Pig

Apple tree

Sheep

## Working the design

**4** Press under the edges of the sections. Baste them to the interfacing background, edges touching. Set the sewing machine to a zigzag and work round the pieces, except the outside edges. Straight-stitch round the outside edges.

**5** Stitch white ricrac braid around section 2. Stitch pieces of green ricrac braid to section 6. Embroider grass in straight and fly stitches.

**6** Work cream detached chain and fly stitches over section 8. Work white straight stitch clouds on section 9 and white French knot flowers with green fly stitch leaves on section 4.

**7** Draw 10 circles 1¼in (3cm) diameter on white felt and embroider the numerals 1–10 in black chain stitches. Cut out and slipstitch each numbered circle to its section.

Scale: 1 sq = 1in (2.5cm)

**8** FIGURES AND ANIMALS: Place felt pieces together with the beige shape at the back and oversew together, leaving a gap. Stuff, close the gap. Embroider the details (features etc) and then sew on the animal's heads. Cut small pieces of touch-and-hold fastening and sew one side to the backs of the figures, animals and birds. Sew the other side to the farmyard sections (refer to the picture).

## Finishing

**9** Fold the edges of the backing fabric to the wrong side. Slipstitch to the back along the top edge. Machine-stitch 1½in (4cm) below to make a casing for the rod. Slipstitch the backing to the panel all round. Insert the dowelling. Tie the ribbon ends to the dowelling.

---

### Sewing on trimmings
**Ricrac braid** Machine-stitch to the fabric working down the middle of the braid.
**Ribbon** Machine-stitch down both edges, working in the same direction.

---

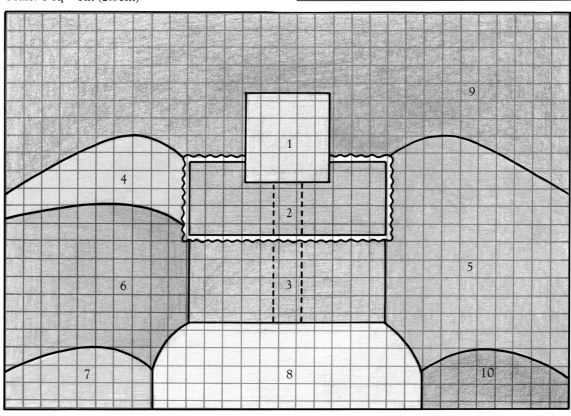

# Rocking hen toy

*Simple woodworking skills are all that this cheerful toy requires. The decoration provides scope for using bright colours which all small children love.*

### Materials

Squared pattern paper
7ft (2.15m) of ¾in (2cm)-thick pine wood
6in (15cm) of ½in (1cm) ramin dowelling
Sandpaper in coarse, medium and fine
   grades
Wood glue
8 countersunk wood screws, 1¼in (3.5cm)
2in (5cm) countersunk wood screw
Wood filler
Craft paints, yellow, red, white, blue and
   black
Satin finish polyurethane varnish

### Preparation

1 Draw the patterns on squared paper.
Mark the arrows to indicate the grain of
wood. Using the patterns, mark on the
wood 2 rockers, 2 side heads, 1 centre
head and 1 tail. Mark 1 seat piece with
the back end of the seat (A-B) cut at a 45°
angle (see pattern). Cut 1 front section.

### Working the design

2 Cut the various pieces.

3 HEAD: Smooth the edges of the head
with sandpaper. Glue together the three
sections and, when the glue is dry, level
up the back and front edge, sandpapering
as necessary. Square up the lower end of
the neck and make any adjustments by
planing or sawing to ensure that the head
stands upright. Sandpaper the head
thoroughly and make a chamfer on all
edges except at the bottom where the
head fits the body.

4 HANDLES: Using a ½in (1cm) bit, drill a
¾in (18mm) hole on each side of the head
(at x on the pattern). Cut 2 pieces of
ramin dowelling each 2¾in (7cm) long and
stick a piece into each hole for handles.

5 BODY: Glue together the seat, rockers
and front section, making sure that the
angled edge of the seat is at the back,
where the tail will fit later. The front end
of the seat fits flush to the front of the
rockers and the front section. Square up
the fit of the various sections and leave
the glue to dry, under clamps if possible.

6 At the top of each rocker, drill 4 pilot
holes to take the 1¼in (3.5cm) screws.
They should be at a depth of ⅜in (9mm)
from the straight edge and evenly spaced.
The screws are countersunk so that the
heads are below the wood surface.

7 The last screw at either end will hold
the tail. Apply glue to the end of the seat
and stick the tail in place, then insert the
screws. Fill the countersunk holes with
wood filler.

### Finishing

8 Sandpaper the toy thoroughly and
chamfer the edges. Stick the head to the
centre front of the body. When the glue
is dry drill a pilot hole and screw the
head to the body from the inside of the
work, using the remaining screw.

9 Dilute the craft paints with water,
paint the toy, following the picture.
Finish with a coat of polyurethane
varnish.

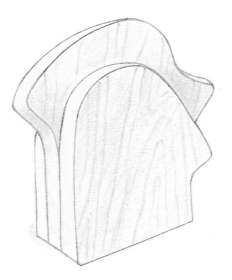

Glue the three head sections together.

Scale: 1 sq = 2in (5cm)

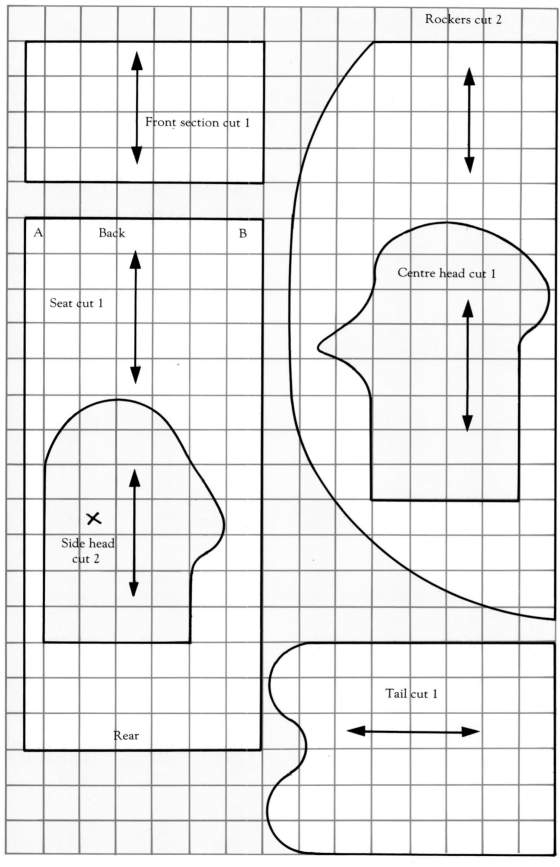

Rockers cut 2

Front section cut 1

A      Back      B

Seat cut 1

Centre head cut 1

✕

Side head
cut 2

Rear

Tail cut 1

# Fishy play mat

*Baby will enjoy taking his exercise among the fishes on this colourful mat. It provides both interest and play. There is a starfish puppet also so that you can join in the fun.*

## Materials
Squared pattern paper, thin cardboard
45 × 45in (115 × 115cm) piece of dark
   cotton fabric (background)
Scraps of brightly coloured cotton fabrics
11 × 40in (28 × 102cm) piece of towelling
   (for puppet)
19½ × 39in (50 × 100cm) patterned or plain
   fabric (sea)
Scraps of felt
2 toy squeakers
Small, round mirror
4in (10cm) piece of touch-and-hold
   fastening
Washable polyester toy filling
5 small bells
Narrow ribbon
3 round, plastic boxes with lids
Pebbles or beads
Self-adhesive fabric tape
Stranded embroidery cottons
8 × 16in (20 × 40cm) piece of heavyweight
   non-woven interfacing
19½ × 39in (50 × 100cm) piece of fabric
   (shore)
5 buttons
10 × 15in (25 × 38cm) piece of felt
3¼in (3m) of wide, white ricrac braid
39in (100cm) square of backing fabric

## Preparation
**1** Draw the patterns on squared paper.
Transfer (or stick) the patterns to
cardboard and cut out for templates.

**2** Cut the background fabric to 39in
(100cm) square.

**3** Place the fish templates on the wrong
side of the coloured fabrics and draw
round 5 fish bodies and 7 tails. Cut out,
allowing an extra ¼in (6mm) seam

allowance all round. For 2 squeaky fish,
cut 2 pairs of bodies in each of two
colours, again adding seam allowance.

**4** For the starfish puppet, use the
templates to cut 2 starfish bodies from
towelling, adding seam allowance all
round. Cut 2 glove shapes also.

## Working the design
**5** THE SEA: Place the cardboard
templates on the wrong side of the fish
shapes and press the seam allowance to
the wrong side. Remove the templates.

**6** Lightly chalk an area of 15 × 24in
(38 × 60cm) in the centre of the sea fabric,
then arrange the fish in the area. Baste the
7 fish tails down first, then the 5 fish
bodies, overlapping the tails. (Two tails
are for the squeaker fish later.) Zigzag
stitch all round the fish then work 2
vertical stripes along each. (Use a
decorative stitch if your machine has one.
Otherwise, work the stripes by hand.)
Sew felt circles to the fish for eyes.

**7** SQUEAKER FISH: On the remaining fish
pieces, work 2 stripes along one body
piece of each. Stitch a 2in (5cm) strip of
touch-and-hold fastening down the
middle of the corresponding shape. With
right sides facing, join the shapes, leaving
a gap. Turn to the right side, stuff lightly,
inserting a squeaker, and close the gap.
Stitch the corresponding lengths of
touch-and-hold fastening next to the tails
where the squeaky fish are to be
positioned.

**8** STARFISH PUPPET: Stitch the glove
pieces together, leaving the wrist edge

open. Neaten all raw edges. Stitch the pieces of starfish together, leaving a gap. Turn to the right side, stuff lightly and close the gap. Sew felt eyes to the face and embroider a mouth.

**9** Pin the starfish to the glove, matching fingers and starfish arms, then sew in place. Sew a bell to each starfish arm. Sew a ribbon loop to the top arm.

**10** PEBBLE RATTLES: Put pebbles (or beads) into the flat, round boxes and tape

the lids on securely. Cut 2 felt circles (use pinking shears if you have them) 4½in (11cm) diameter, for each box. Sew felt eyes and embroider a mouth to the centre of one circle. Top-stitch the circles together, close to the edges.

**11** To stuff the rattles, cut a slit down the centre of the back, insert the plastic container and stuff round the edges to pad. Close the slit with oversewing. Sew a ribbon loop at top centre to fit a button later.

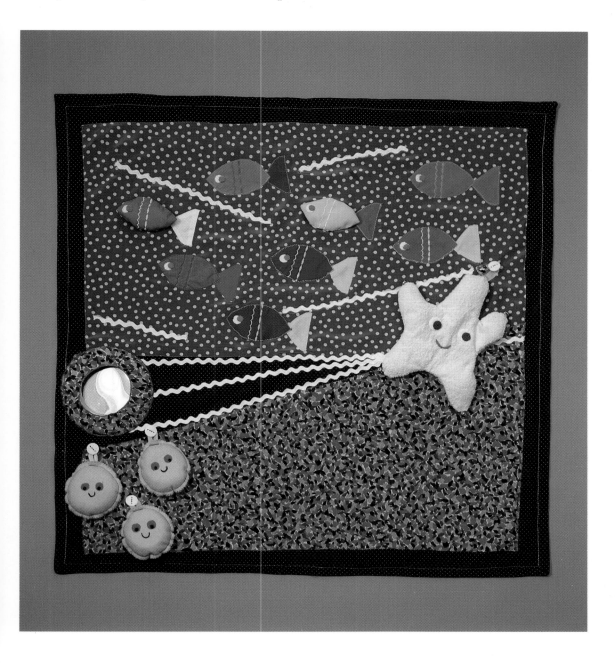

Scale: 1 sq = 1in (2.5cm)

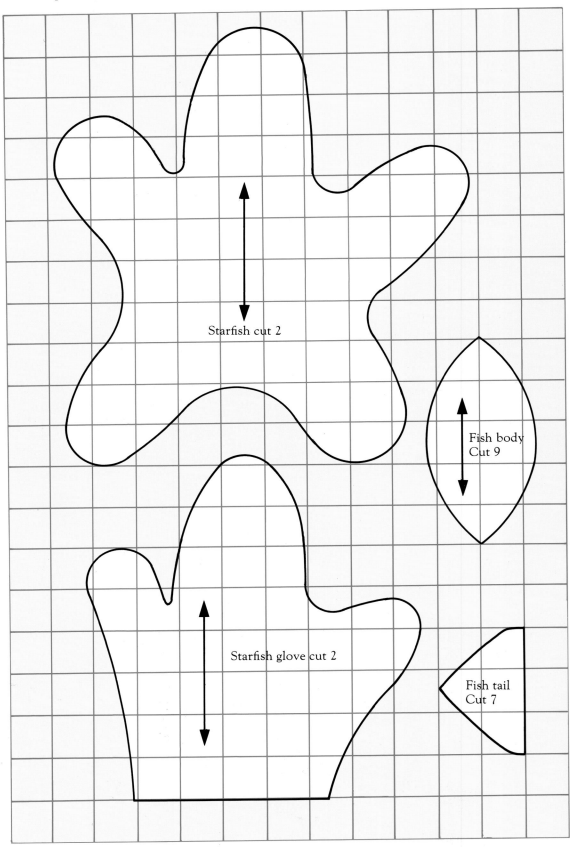

Starfish cut 2

Fish body
Cut 9

Starfish glove cut 2

Fish tail
Cut 7

**12** ROCK POOL: For the upper covering of the pool, cut an 8in (20cm) circle of heavy-weight non-woven interfacing. Mark and then cut a circle from the centre 4½in (11cm) diameter.

**13** Next, from the shore fabric, cut 2 circles 8¾in (22cm) diameter. Right sides facing, stitch them together, leaving a gap for turning. Turn right side out. Insert the prepared interfacing and oversew the gap. Pin the inner edges of the fabric to the edges of the hole in the interfacing. Snip a 3½in (9cm) diameter circle through both thicknesses of fabric. Snip into the edges, fold to the wrong side and oversew to neaten.

**14** Gather the outer and inner edges. Draw up the outer gathering so that the diameter is contracted to 7in (18cm). Draw up the inner gathering a little.

**15** ROCK POOL BACKING: Cut a 7in (18cm) circle of interfacing and cover with fabric in the same way as stages 12 and 13. Oversew the upper covering edges to the backing, leaving a gap for inserting the mirror. Make a thread loop for a button to close the gap.

**16** Pin and baste the sea and shore to the background fabric, allowing a margin all round. Leave a horizontal, v-shaped space (refer to picture) so that the background fabric shows between the sea and the shore (about 7in (18cm) at the left-hand end). Cut the shore at an angle, turn a

narrow hem, top-stitch the shore to the background.

**17** Cut and stitch 3 pieces of white ricrac braid to the fabric between sea and shore. Cut the remaining braid into short pieces and stitch between the fish. Sew the rock pool to the shore.

**18** Sew on the buttons to hold the pebble rattles and the starfish puppet. Wrong sides facing, baste the background edges and backing fabric together. From the remaining background fabric, cut 4 facing strips each 3 × 39in (7.5 × 100cm) and face the edges of the play mat.

**19** On the front, fold and stitch the facing edges in place.

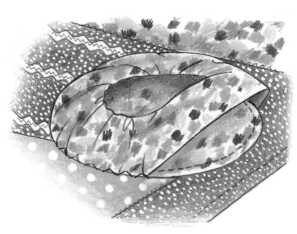

Oversew the upper covering to the backing, leaving a gap for the mirror.

# Tiny toys

*These pretty little toys, a bunny, a pussy and a teddy,*
*are just the right size for a baby's hand and use only small pieces*
*of washable fabric.*

**Materials**
For each toy
Tracing pattern paper
8 × 12in (20 × 30cm) piece of soft fabric
5 × 9in (13 × 23cm) piece of patterned
   cotton fabric
Small pieces of washable fun felt
Stranded embroidery cottons
Washable polyester toy filling
**In addition for the bunny**
4 × 5in (10 × 13cm) piece of contrasting
   cotton fabric
1 small button
**In addition for the teddy**
2 small buttons

**Preparation**
**1** Trace the pattern pieces for the toy.
Cut out and put in all the markings.
Seam allowances of $\frac{1}{4}$in (6mm) are
included.

**2** Fold the soft fabric in half widthways,
right sides facing. Pin the body pattern to
the doubled fabric and cut out. Mark the
position 'X' on one body (see pattern).
Pin the ear pattern (teddy, pussy or
bunny) to doubled soft fabric and cut
out. Pin the ear pattern to doubled
patterned fabric and cut 2 ear linings. Cut
eyes and noses from felt.

**Bunny**
**3** From patterned fabric, cut 1 waistcoat
back and 2 waistcoat fronts. Cut the
same pieces from contrasting cotton. Cut
a 1$\frac{1}{2}$in (37mm)-diameter circle of soft
fabric for the tail.

**Pussy**
**4** From the patterned fabric, cut a skirt
piece 2 × 9in (5 × 23cm) and a bias-cut
strip 1$\frac{1}{2}$ × 6in (3 × 15cm) for a bow.

**Trace these pattern pieces**

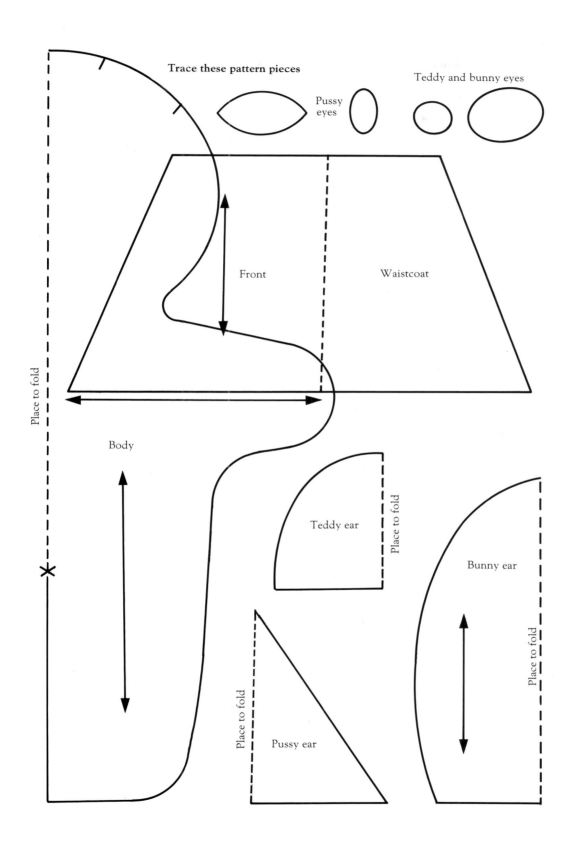

Pussy eyes

Teddy and bunny eyes

Place to fold

Front

Waistcoat

Body

Teddy ear

Place to fold

Bunny ear

Place to fold

Place to fold

Pussy ear

**Teddy**

**5** From patterned fabric, cut a piece for the trousers, 2 × 6½in (5 × 16cm). Cut a bib front 1½ × 3in (3 × 7.5cm) and 2 straps each 1 × 4in (2.5 × 10cm).

**Working the design**

**6** EARS: For the bunny and teddy, baste a soft fabric ear to a patterned ear, right sides facing. Stitch round the curved edge, clip into the seam allowance and turn right side out. For the pussy, stitch along 2 straight sides.

**7** With the patterned side of the ear facing you, fold the outer corners to the centre and baste to the right side of one body piece (see pattern).

**8** Right sides facing, baste the body pieces together from A to D. Machine-stitch but do not turn yet.

**9** LEGS: Mark a line on the toy body from the mark 'X' to the bottom edge. Machine-stitch on either side ⅛in (3mm) from the line. Cut along the line. Turn the toy right side out and stuff lightly. Close the gap in the seam.

**Finishing**

**10** Sew the eyes and nose to the face. Embroider the mouth, using all 6 strands of embroidery cotton together. Add whiskers to the bunny and pussy using 2 strands of embroidery cotton.

**11** BUNNY: Gather the edges of the tail circle and draw up tightly. Stuff lightly and sew to the back of the toy. With right sides facing, stitch the patterned fabric waistcoat to the contrasting fabric pieces, leaving a gap to turn. Turn to the right side and press. Pin the back and front to the toy and catch the shoulders and lower, outside corners together. Overlap the fronts at the inner corners. Sew a button in place.

**12** TEDDY: On the trousers strip, press ¼in (6mm) to the wrong side on the long edges. Stitch. Join the short ends at the centre back and work a ½in (1cm)-wide slit for the legs (refer back to stage 9). Turn to the right side.

**13** With right sides facing, fold the bib front in half, stitch round, leaving a gap and turn to the right side. Catch the unstitched edge to underlap the centre front edge of the trousers.

**14** STRAPS: Press ¼in (6mm) to the wrong side on the long edges then fold the strips in half lengthways. Stitch along the edges. Catch the straps under the top of the bib front. Sew on the buttons. Slip the trousers on the teddy, cross the straps at the back and catch the ends to the back of the trousers.

**15** PUSSY: Turn a narrow hem on the long edges of the skirt and join the short ends. Gather one long edge, draw up to fit the toy and catch in place. Make a bow from the bias strip (refer to stage 14 for the teddy straps). Sew the bow to the front.

---

**Enlarging patterns**

Trace-off patterns can be made larger (or smaller) simply by turning them into graph patterns. First, trace the pattern from the page. Rule lines round the shapes so that they are in a square or rectangular box. Measure and mark the box outline into 1in (2.5cm) squares.

Next, decide the size you want to enlarge the pattern to. Draw a box outline to the dimensions. Measure and mark the outline into the same number of squares as your original pattern. Then, all you have to do is copy the pattern outlines into each of the squares.

You can reduce a pattern in the same way. Simply draw a boxed area to the smaller dimensions, mark the box into the same number of squares as your original pattern, and then copy the pattern into the squares.

# Push-along pigeon

*This unusual toy was inspired by the way real pigeons move their heads as they walk. You could try the pattern first in strong cardboard before making the toy in wood.*

Scale: 1 sq = ½in (1cm)

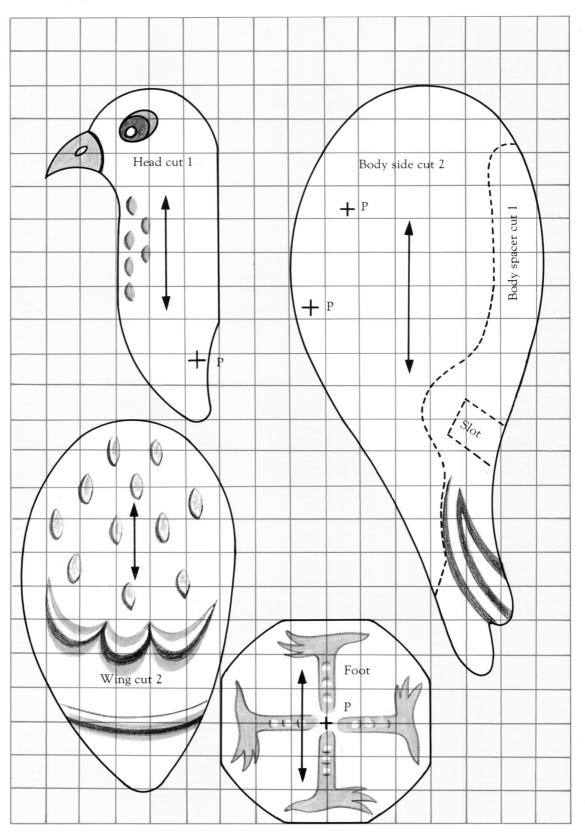

Head cut 1

Body side cut 2

+ P

+ P

Body spacer cut 1

+ P

Slot

Wing cut 2

Foot

+ P

## Materials

Squared pattern paper

$6 \times 7$in ($15 \times 18$cm) piece of $\frac{1}{8}$in (3mm)
  birch ply-wood for wings

$8\frac{3}{4} \times 13$in ($22 \times 33$cm) piece of $\frac{1}{4}$in (6mm)
  birch plywood for other parts

39in (1m) of $\frac{5}{8}$in (15mm) diameter
  dowelling for a handle

4in (10cm) thin, stiff wire

Empty plastic food pot

Fine sandpaper; wood glue

Modeller's enamel paint

## Preparation

**1** Draw the pattern pieces on squared
paper. Mark the pivot points (P)
accurately.

**2** Trace 2 wings onto the $\frac{1}{8}$in (3mm) ply-
wood. Trace 2 bodies and one each of the
other shapes on $\frac{1}{4}$in (6mm) ply-wood.
Mark 2 pivot points on the outer
surfaces of the bodies (reversing one
body so that you have a pair). Mark
spacer positions on the inner surfaces of
the feet wheel and the head.

## Working the design

**3** Cut out all the shapes and lightly
sandpaper the edges. Sandpaper the outer
surfaces only of the 2 bodies and wings
(reversing to give a pair). Sandpaper both
surfaces of the head and feet wheel so
that they are very smooth (they must fit
loosely between the body pieces).

**4** Drill the pivot holes. (Check that the
wire turns easily through the holes. If it
seems tight, use a drill bit slightly larger.)

**5** Paint one surface and the edges of the
body and wing pieces, making sure that
you reverse them to make a pair. On the
body spacer, paint the edge only. Using
the wood glue, stick the inside of the
wings to the outside of the bodies.

**6** Cut 4 washers from the plastic food
pot each $\frac{1}{2}$in (1cm) diameter. Use these on
the pivot wires on each side of the
moving parts.

Here is how the pigeon fits together. As the
wheel rotates it makes the head move
back and forth.

**7** Cut 2 pivot wires each $\frac{3}{4}$in (18mm)
long. Push the wires through the drilled
holes on one body side so that they
project on the inside. Place the head and
feet wheel over the pivots. Hold the body
side vertically and check that rotating the
wheel moves the head to and fro.

**8** Hold the body spacer in position on
the same body piece. Check that the head
still moves freely. When you are
satisfied, the spacer may be stuck to the
inside of the body piece. Fit the other
side of the body over the pivot wires.
Hold the body firmly together and check
that the head and feet wheel move freely.
Any slight stiffness can be reduced by
sanding them down a little more.

**9** Remove the head and the feet wheel
and paint them. When completely dry,
replace them in position. Stick the
second body piece in place.

## Finishing

**10** Shape the end of the handle and stick
the end into the slot in the body spacer.

# Geese pram toy

*Babies will love this little toy, fixed across the pram or crib. Use washable, colourfast felt for the beaks, feet and eyes. You could string coloured wooden beads between the geese.*

## Materials
Tracing pattern paper
6 × 36in (15 × 90cm) piece of white cotton towelling
Washable polyester toy filling
8in (20cm) square of orange fun felt
Scraps of blue fun felt
White stranded embroidery cotton

1yd (1m) approximately of ⅛in (3mm)-wide satin ribbon
Round elastic (optional)

## Preparation
1 Trace the pattern on pattern paper. Cut out the body and wing pieces have ¼in (6mm) seam allowances included.

**Trace these pattern pieces.**

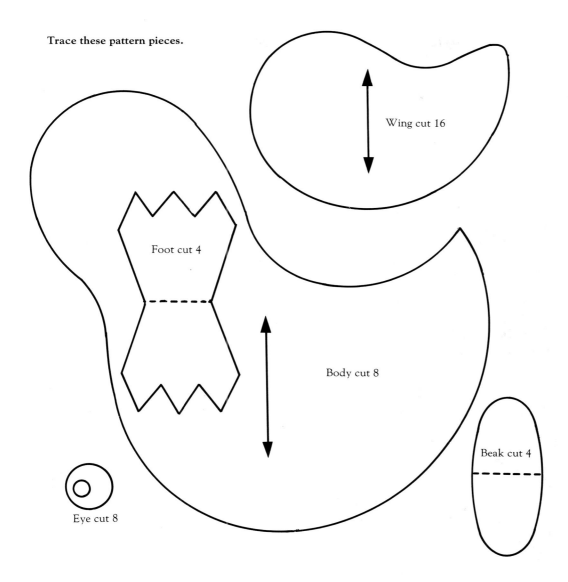

Wing cut 16

Foot cut 4

Body cut 8

Beak cut 4

Eye cut 8

**2** Pin the patterns to fabric and cut out 8 bodies and 16 wings. From orange fun felt, cut 4 beaks and 4 pairs of feet. From blue fun felt, cut 8 circles for eyes.

**Working the design**
**3** Stitch the bodies together in pairs, right sides facing, leaving a gap for turning. Turn to the right side and stuff lightly. Close the gaps.

**4** Make up the wings in the same way but do not stuff. Sew the wings to the bodies.

**5** Fold the beaks and feet in half and sew to the bodies so that 2 geese face to the right and 2 face to the left. Sew on the eyes and embroider a French knot on each eye.

**6** Thread the ribbon on a sharp, large-eyed needle. Pass the needle through each of the geese. Attach elastic loops to the ends if desired.

# Caterpillar toy

*A colourful pull-along toy that will delight any toddler. You will enjoy making it because only very simple woodcraft techniques are involved.*

## Materials
Glass paper
11in (28cm) piece of 2⅛ × 1¾in (3 × 4.5cm) pine (body)
1¾in (4.5cm) square of pine wood (head)
8in (20cm) piece of pine, ⅝ × ⅝in (15mm × 15mm)
18in (45cm) length of expanding curtain wire
Wood glue
7in (18cm) piece of 1in (2.5cm) dowelling
24in (60cm) piece of ¼in (6mm) dowelling
2 smaller beads (nose and tail)
Modeller's enamel paints
Small screw eye
11 large, coloured wooden beads
Cord

## Preparation
**1** Smooth off all the pieces of wood.

**2** Round off the edges of the body piece of wood then cut into nine 1¼in (3cm) pieces. Round off the edges of the head piece.

**3** Drill a hole through the centre of one of the 9 body pieces, so that the curtain wire slips through easily. Hold the drilled piece against an undrilled piece and mark the position of the hole with the drill bit. Drill all the pieces with a hole. Number the pieces as you drill them.

**4** Drill a hole about ¾in (18mm) deep in the centre of one side of the head piece. Drill 2 holes diagonally into the front top edge of the head piece for inserting the feelers later.

**5** Take the third piece of wood and, starting ⅝in (15mm) from one end, drill 6 holes to take the ¼in (6mm) dowelling loosely. Space each so that it is 1⅛in (3cm) away from the previous hole. Saw the wood into 9 1⅛in (3cm) pieces so that a hole is in the centre of each.

**6** String the body pieces on the curtain wire temporarily and decide which of the sides will be the under body. Stick one of the drilled pieces you prepared in stage 5 underneath each of five body segments. Stick one under the head segment. Remove the pieces from the wire.

**7** WHEELS: Cut 12 wheels ⅜in (1cm) thick from the 1in (2.5cm) dowelling. Smooth with glass paper. Drill a ¼in (6mm) hole through the centre of each. Using pencil compasses, draw a 1in (2.5cm) circle on paper. Cut out and use this as a pattern to mark the centre of the wheels. Paint the wheels.

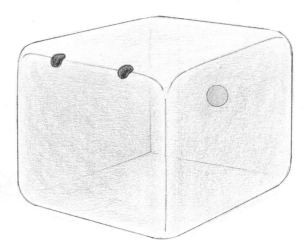

Drill a hole about ¾in (18mm) deep in one side of the head piece. Drill holes for the two feelers.

**8** Cut 6 pieces each 2¾in (7cm) from the ¼in (6mm) dowelling. Stick a wheel on one end of each piece. Thread the dowel through the hole under the body pieces and the head piece. Stick on the other wheel.

**9** HEAD: Paint the toy. Paint the face. Stick on a bead for the nose. Insert the screw eye in the lower front. Cut two 2¾in (7cm) pieces of dowelling and stick them into the holes in the head. Stick beads onto the ends for feelers.

**10** Glue a small bead onto one end of the curtain wire for a tail. Thread on a wheeled body piece, a bead and then a body piece in that order to the head. Stick the wire end into the drilled head. Attach a cord to the screw eye.

Cut two wheels, drill holes in the centre. Stick a wheel on one end of the dowel.

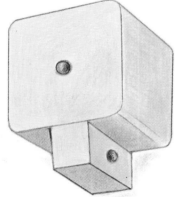

Cut six underbody pieces with a hole drilled in each.

Stick the drilled underbody pieces under the body segments

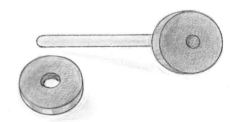

# Swings mobile

*Boys and girls come out to play under the tree on this innovative mobile. It is a simple and inexpensive toy to make, mostly using scraps of coloured paper and knitting wool.*

## Materials
Squared pattern paper
Thin cardboard for templates
9 × 10in (23 × 25cm) piece of stiff, thin cardboard
9 × 20in (23 × 50cm) piece of green felt
Small pieces of stiff paper, white, blue, yellow, red, peach and light brown
Brown and yellow knitting wool
Red and blue felt-tipped pens
Adhesive
1yd (1m) approximately ½in (1cm)-wide green satin ribbon
9 red beads, 9 green beads
Green pearl cotton
Wire paper clip

## Preparation
1 Draw the patterns for the tree and dolls' tops on squared paper. Stick to thin card and cut out for templates.

2 For the tree, cut 2 shapes from cardboard and 4 from green felt.

3 For the boy dolls, cut 5 tops from white paper. Cut 5 blue paper strips each 1⅛in × 11in (3 × 28cm) for trousers.

4 For the girl dolls, cut 2 dresses from red paper and 2 dresses from yellow paper. Cut 2in (5cm) circles for under the dolls, 2 yellow and 2 red.

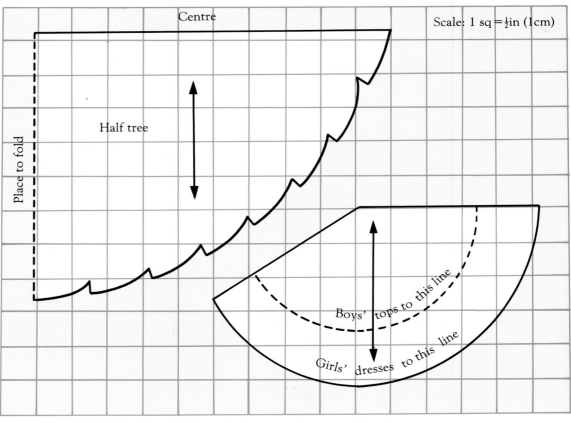

**5** For the heads, cut 9 strips of pink paper ¾ × 6in (18 mm × 15cm). For the arms cut 5 strips of white paper, 2 of red paper and 2 of yellow, each 3⅜ × ½in (8.5 × 1cm). Cut ½in (1cm)-long pieces of pink paper for hands. Stick to the ends of the arms and then round off the corners for hands. For the legs, cut 9 strips of pink paper 3⅜ × ½in (8.5 × 1cm).

**6** Curl the garments pieces and heads by pulling them over a knife blade.

**7** SWINGS: Cut 9 strips of cardboard, each 1 × 2½in (2.5 × 6cm). Stick light brown paper to both sides to make the swings seats. For the swing ropes, cut 9 strips of light brown paper each ⅜ × 11in (9mm × 28cm).

## Working the design

**8** TREE: Stick the felt shapes to each side of the cardboard. Cut leaf-shaped holes at random in each 'branch'. Cut the curved edges into leaf shapes. To assemble the tree, cut a slot in both pieces, on one from the curved edge, and from the straight edge on the other. Push the two pieces together at right angles. Pierce holes at the intersection, using a thick needle. Pass a piece of stiff wire (such as a straightened paper clip) through the holes and twist the ends to hold the tree shape.

**9** Cut several red paper apples, ½in (1cm) in diameter, and stick them to the tree.

**10** GIRL DOLLS: Roll the dress into a cone shape and stick the straight edges together, overlapping them by ¼in (6mm).

**11** HAIR: Roll the head strip into a tube about ¾in (18mm) diameter and stick over the dress cone point. To make the hair, wind wool 8 times round three fingers. Tie the loops together at the top, stick

the tie inside the top of the head. Stick loops to each side of the head. Draw on the features.

**12** ARMS AND LEGS: Apply adhesive to the middle of the arms piece and stick over the join in the dress. Cut the legs strip into 2 pieces. Colour about ½in (1cm) of one end of each for shoes, then round off the corners. Stick the other ends under the dress hem so that about 1in (2.5cm) protrudes. Bend up the legs, and the shoes. Stick the under-dress circles of paper in place.

**13** BOYS: Roll and stick the paper tops as for the girl's dresses. Roll the trouser strip into a 1in (2.5cm)-diameter tube and stick the overlap. Spread adhesive on the top edge and stick inside the cone top. Roll the head strip, secure and stick over the cone tip. Make hair by winding wool 4 times round two fingers and stick over the top of the head. Draw on the face. Fix the arms and legs in place, as for the girl dolls.

**14** SWINGS: Stick the ends of the rope strip under the ends of the seat.

## Finishing

**15** Sew a ribbon loop to the top middle of the tree to hang the mobile. Holding each swing by the middle of the rope, balance a doll on the seat, then stick in place.

**16** ASSEMBLY: Tie a green bead to the end of an 18in (45cm) length of thread. Pass the other end into a needle. Push the needle upwards through the middle of the swing rope, then through the tree centre and through a red bead. Tie the thread loosely, adjust the length to about 12in (30cm). This will be the longest thread of the mobile.

**17** Fasten the other swings in the same way, varying the length of thread and adjusting the threads to balance the mobile. Secure thread ends with a dab of adhesive.

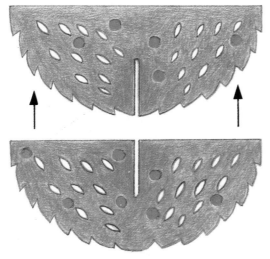

Fit the two tree pieces together on the slots.

# Fabric and ribbons basket

*This woven basket is ideal for filling with small gifts for a new baby. Afterwards, it can be used in the nursery for creams, powders, tissues and wipes etc.*

## Materials

18 × 45in (45 × 115cm) piece of finely woven cotton fabric

18 × 45in (45 × 115cm) piece of thin wadding

5 × 31in (13 × 80cm) piece of white cotton

3yd (2.80cm) velvet ribbon, ¼in (6mm) wide

30in (75cm) of 1in (2.5cm)-wide broderie anglaise edging

7 × 21in (18 × 53cm) of heavyweight non-woven interfacing

## Preparation

1 Cut a piece of printed fabric to 18 × 28in (45 × 70cm) and a piece of wadding to the same size. Baste them together on the edges.

2 To make the weaving strips for the basket sides, the fabric is stitched to the wadding, then cut into strips. Using a ruler and chalk (or a washable fabric pen), mark the fabric on the right side, starting ¼in (6mm) from one long edge. Mark off 2½in (6cm) sections with ½in (1cm) between each section.

3 Cut 2 circles of interfacing each 6¼in (16cm) diameter for the basket base. Baste them together on the edges. Cut another circle of interfacing for the lining, this time 5½in (13cm) diameter.

## Working the design

4 On the marked, mounted fabric stitch along the marked lines. Cut the fabric into 6 strips along the centre of the ½in (1cm) spaces.

5 With the wadding on the inside, fold the strips lengthways, matching raw edges, then stitch again over the previous row of stitching. Bring the seam to the centre and press, very lightly, without flattening the wadding.

6 WEAVING THE BASKET: Work on an ironing board or a padded surface. Cut a piece of scrap fabric 5 × 2in (12.5 × 5cm). Baste, then stitch the end of each padded strip to this, spacing them so that together they measure 4½in (11cm) across. The seams should be face down. Pin the spare fabric down firmly.

7 Pin one end of the ribbon to the top of the right-hand strip and weave the end under and over the strips to the left. Bring the ribbon over the left-hand strip, twisting it to the right side and continue weaving to the right. The ribbons should lie about 1in (2.5cm) apart.

**8** Continue weaving until the work measures about 21in (53cm) long. (You may have a surplus of the padded strips at the end.) Catch the ribbon end to the wrong side of the weaving.

**9** ASSEMBLING THE BASKET: Baste, then stitch across the end of the weaving. Cut off the surplus within ¼in (6mm) of the weaving. Right sides facing, join the short ends. Turn to the right side. To attach the base, pin the 2 circles of interfacing, together, to the wrong side of the printed cotton fabric and cut out with 1in (2.5cm) all round. Pin the smaller interfacing circle to the white fabric, cut out with 1in (2.5cm) all round. Clip into the edges, turn the tabs to the wrong side and baste.

**10** Pin the basket to the base and sew the base in place, working from the outside, and working the stitches through the ribbon only. Gather the broderie anglaise and fit it round the inside top of the basket. Slipstitch in place and oversew the cut ends.

**11** HANDLE: From the remaining printed fabric, cut and make 3 more strips, as you did for the basket sides strips, each 18in (45cm) long. Plait the strips together tightly, baste, then stitch across the ends, trimming any surplus. Sew the ends to the inside top of the basket sides.

**12** LINING: Cut a piece of lining fabric 5 × 21in (13 × 53cm). Right sides facing, join the short ends, turn to the right side. Press a ½in (1cm) hem to the wrong side on the top edge and gather, just under the folded edge. Gather within ½in (1cm) of the lower edge. Pull up the top gathering to fit inside the basket and then pull up the lower gathering. Place the lining in the basket and catch the upper edge over the broderie anglaise trimming and the handle ends.

**13** Insert the lining-covered interfacing circle. Remove all basting.

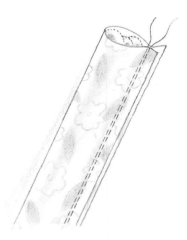

Wadding on the inside, match raw edges and stitch the strip again.

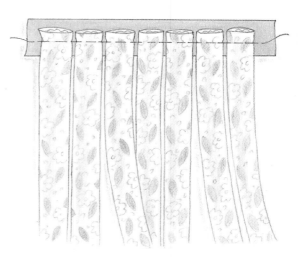

Baste and stitch the strips to the fabric scrap.

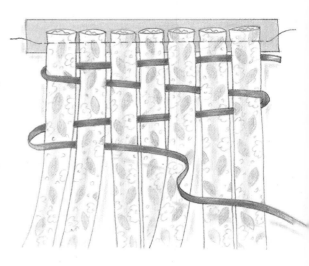

Starting at the right-hand side, weave under and over the strips to the left.

# Keepsakes box

*Most mothers treasure little mementoes of their babies. Decorate a special box with a painted design to keep the mementoes together. It makes a delightful new baby gift.*

**Trace, or use this graph pattern as required**

## Materials
Tracing or squared pattern paper
Wooden box with a top approximately
   7 × 10in (18 × 25cm), stripped and
   sanded smooth
Wood primer, fine sandpaper
Crafts paints; matt varnish

## Preparation
1 Paint the box with primer. When dry,
smooth down with fine sandpaper.

2 The box pictured was painted first with
deep blue paint, then a coat of turquoise.
The final coat of turquoise was mixed
with a little white and a touch of black.
Paint was applied roughly so that
previous coats showed through a little.
Paint can be wiped from corners and
edges to give an 'antiqued' look. Paint the
inside edges of the box and lid.

## Working the design
3 Trace the patterns on pattern paper.
(Alternatively, enlarge the graph pattern
as required.) Transfer the designs to the
box top and sides. Paint the design,
following the picture. Paint the central
oval white with a dark, outer shadow and
add the baby's initials.

4 Varnish the box all over.

### Lining boxes
Measure the box sides, the lid and
the base. Draw the shapes onto thin
card. Draw a second line ¼in (6mm)
inside the outline. Place the card
pieces on medium-weight interfacing.
Trace round twice. Cut out, adding
¼in (6mm) all round. Stick the
interfacings to each side of the card
pieces, turning the edges in.
   Place the covered card pieces on
fabric. Trace round. Cut out, adding
¼in (6mm) all round. Place the fabric
on the right side of the covered
pieces, stick down the turnings on
the wrong side. Stick the lining
pieces to the inside of the box.

# Teddy bear découpage jar

*An ordinary jam or jelly jar can be transformed into a useful and attractive accessory with just cut-out paper motifs, adhesive and paint – plus, of course, a ribbon bow!*

**Materials**
Glass jar (or other container)
Motifs for cutting out
PVA water-soluble adhesive
Modeller's paint
Ribbon trimming

**Preparation**
1 Wash the jar thoroughly making sure that any residue of label glue is removed. Dry and polish the jar with a warm dry cloth.

2 Using curved nail scissors, cut out motifs. Take great care at this stage because careful cutting out is the secret of good découpage. Hold the scissors so that the blades curve towards your body and cut with little 'feathering' movements so that the edge is slightly serrated. (This helps the paper to adhere more firmly when it is stuck down.)

**Working the design**
3 Spread adhesive very thinly on the front of the motif, right up to the edges. Position the motif on the inside of the jar, front side to the glass.

4 Smooth out any air bubbles with a finger tip. Make sure the motif is stuck down to the glass on all the edges. Remove any excess adhesive that seeps out with a dampened cotton wool bud. Leave to dry.

5 Use the paint fairly thick and only have a little on the brush tip. Dab paint over the inside of the glass, working very slowly and carefully. Use as little paint as possible for this first coat. Paint all over the back of the motif. Leave to dry.

6 Dab on a second coat if the découpage seems to need it. Finish the jar with a ribbon bow.

Dab paint carefully on the inside of the jar, covering the glass and the back of the motifs.

# Ducks cross stitch picture

*This charming nursery picture is so simple that it could be worked in an evening for a last-minute gift. The standing duck motif could also be embroidered on a bought feeder or a little dress.*

### Materials
Piece of white Aida fabric, 12 holes to
   1in (2.5cm)
Stranded embroidery cottons, dark
   yellow, orange, mid-green, pale green,
   blue and black

### Preparation
1 Mark the middle of the fabric with basting threads, horizontally and vertically. Count squares on the chart and mark the middle of it.

### Working the design
2 Following the colour chart, work the design in cross stitches, using 2 strands of thread together, and starting in the middle of the chart.

3 Work the eyes in three-quarter cross stitches (or, if you prefer, work French knots using black cotton.

4 Press the finished embroidery on the wrong side. Mount the embroidery on a self-adhesive mounting board, and trim to size for framing.

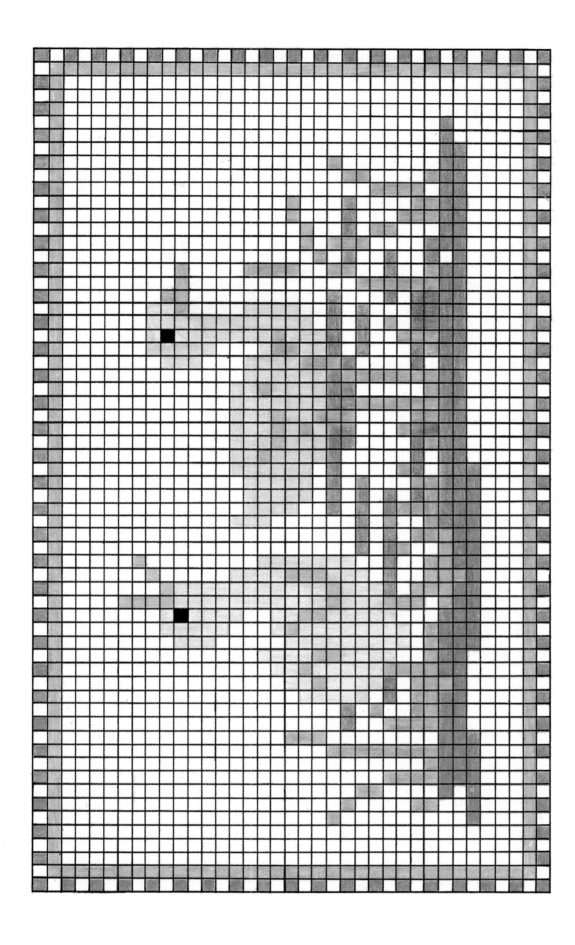

# Cat tissue box cover

*Pretty box covers are welcome gifts and this one makes an amusing addition to the nursery. The measurements are for a small rectangular box but you could adapt them to a larger box.*

## Materials

For a box approximately 5½ × 9 × 3in
  (13 × 23 × 7.5cm)
Tracing paper
21 × 15in (30 × 38cm) piece of patterned
  fabric
12 × 25in (30 × 65cm) piece of plain fabric
12 × 15in (30 × 38cm) piece of thin,
  polyester wadding
6 × 12in (15 × 30cm) piece of white fabric
  (pillow and sheet)
Small piece of fluffy, beige fabric
Small piece of fluffy, pink fabric
Scraps of felt, pink, dark grey
Stranded embroidery cottons
Washable polyester toy filling
6in (15cm) of narrow satin ribbon

## Preparation

1  Lay the tissue box on tracing paper and draw round the outline. Fold the pattern twice to mark the middle of each side, then fold again to mark the sides into quarters. Cut out the pattern.

2  Pin the pattern to the middle of the right side of the printed fabric. Draw round the rectangle and mark in the quarters. Unpin the pattern and join the marks, thus making a diamond pattern.

3  Extend the outside lines of the pattern to the edges of the fabric (this will help in making up later).

4  Pin the pattern to the centre of the lining fabric, draw round and then extend the outside lines as you did for the patterned outer fabric. Cut away the corner areas (refer to the pattern).

Machine-stitch the diamond pattern and round the box top. Cut away the corners.

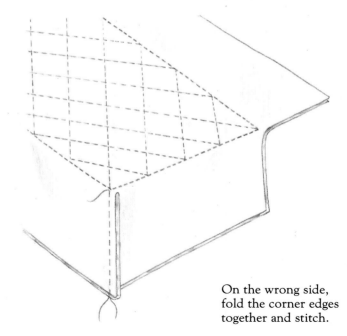

On the wrong side, fold the corner edges together and stitch.

## Working the design

**5** Baste the wadding and outer fabric together round the edges. Machine-quilt along the diamond pattern lines and round the outline of the box top. Cut away the fabric at the corners. Mark a 4in (10cm) line down the centre of the box top for the opening.

**6** CORNERS: On the quilted outer, fold the edges of the cut-away corners together, right sides facing, and machine-stitch. Work the corners of the lining in the same way. Slip the outer onto the lining and pin together. Mark a line 4in (10cm) long down the middle of the top. Using strips of the lining fabric, bind the edges (as you would when making a bound buttonhole). Put the cover on the box and pencil a line round, 1in (2.5cm) above the lower edge of the box. Trim away the fabric up to the line.

**7** Cut the remaining lining fabric into 2¾in (7cm)-wide bias strips. Join strips to make a strip 42in (107cm) long. Fold the strip lengthways, gather up to fit round the box cover. Join the short ends. Baste to the right side of the quilted cover only, matching raw edges. Stitch, taking a ¼in (6mm) seam. Press the edges up on the wrong side of the cover. Fold in the lining edges and slipstitch to the quilted cover.

## Cat and pillow

**8** Trace the patterns for the head, paws and ears. Use the patterns to cut 2 front heads and 1 back head on the fold, 2 ears and 2 paws from the fluffy beige fabric. Cut 2 pink ears and 2 pink paws. (A seam allowance of ¼in (6mm) is included.)

**9** Right sides facing, join the centre front head along A-B then join the front head to the back head (B-C, B-C). Turn the head right side out and stuff. Oversew the neck edges together. Make up 2 ears (pink lined) and 2 paws. Stuff the paws.

**10** Oversew the bottom edges of the paws and ears. Embroider straight stitch claws on the paws. Catch the ears to the head, pink side forwards. Cut a pink felt nose and sew it to the centre front seam of the head. Embroider a pink, smiling mouth in stem stitch and closed, grey eyes. Work the grey whiskers in straight stitches.

**11** PILLOW AND SHEET: Cut a piece of white fabric 6in (15cm) square, fold it across, right sides facing and stitch round, leaving a gap. Turn right side out, stuff lightly and close the gap. Sew the cat head to the pillow along the side seams. Sew the paws either side of the head, just under the pillow edge.

**12** Cut another 6in (15cm) of fabric, fold and stitch as before. Turn but do not stuff. Close the seam. Sew the bottom edge of the pillow to the sheet so that the paws lie on the sheet. Sew the sheet to the box top at one end. Tie a small ribbon bow and sew under the cat's chin.

---

### Adapting the pattern

The little cat head could be adapted to other animals by using a different fabric colour, cutting suitable ears (long ears for a rabbit, round ears for a teddy bear). Or, a small doll's head could be made. Cut the head from pink or beige fabric and embroider closed eyes with eyelashes and a small smiling mouth. Sew doll's hair over the head or you could crochet curls directly onto the fabric.

**Trace these pattern pieces.**

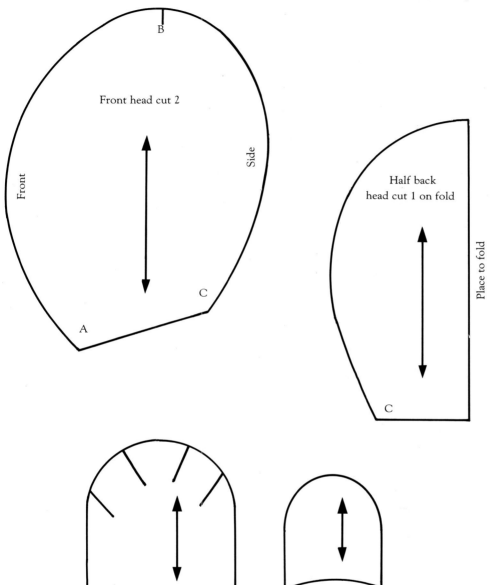

Front head cut 2

Front

Side

B

A

C

Half back
head cut 1 on fold

Place to fold

C

Paw cut 2 from pile fabric,
2 from lining

Ear cut 2 from pile fabric,
2 from lining

# Baby slippers

*These cosy little baby slippers would be welcomed by any mother. The slippers are sized for babies from 6 to 12 months old. Use soft, brushed cotton for the lining.*

**Materials**
Squared pattern paper
28 × 12in (70 × 30cm) piece of outer
 fabric
Lining fabric to the same size
12in (30cm) of thin piping cord
12in (30cm) of 1in (2.5cm)-wide bias
 binding
12in (30cm) of ¼in (6mm)-wide elastic

**Preparation**
**1** Draw the graph pattern on squared
paper (¼in (6mm) seam allowances are
included). Write in all the pattern marks.
Cut out the patterns. Cut out 2 soles, 2
uppers and 2 outers from both the outer
and lining fabrics.

**Working the design**
**2** Baste bias binding round the cord, cut
the covered cord in two. Baste the
binding round the curved edges of the
upper, ½in (1cm) from the edge. Snip into
the seam allowance between A and B.

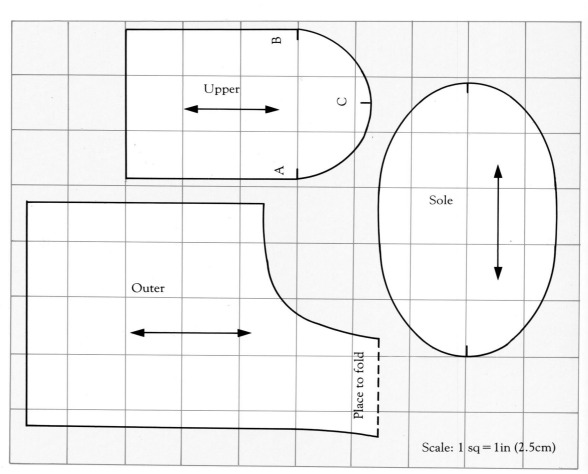

Upper

Outer

Sole

Place to fold

Scale: 1 sq = 1in (2.5cm)

**3** Gather between A and B. Pin C on the upper piece to the centre front outer piece and match the top corners of the upper to the top corners of the outer piece. Baste and stitch, drawing up the gathering as necessary.

**4** Open out the outer slipper; with wrong side facing you, pin one end of the elastic 1¾in (4cm) below the top straight edge at the centre back seam. Pin the other end at the corresponding spot,

stretching the elastic. Machine-stitch along the centre of the elastic. Join the centre back seam. Stitch the sole in place. Make up 2 outer slippers in the same way.

**5** Make up the lining (but without elastic). Turn the outer slipper inside out and slip the lining onto it. Catch the soles together on the seam allowances. Turn in the top edge and slipstitch the lining to the outer.

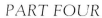
PART FOUR

# Better Techniques

## PATTERN MAKING

The patterns in this book are given in two forms, direct trace-offs and as diagrams. You may sometimes meet another form of pattern – the graph pattern.

Some equipment will be required to prepare patterns for doll making.

### Direct trace-off patterns

To use these, you will need sheets of tracing paper or kitchen greaseproof paper. The tracing paper is laid over the book page and taped down at the edges with small pieces of sticky tape. Trace the image with a sharply-pointed HB pencil.

Very simple shapes may be drawn directly on to the wrong side of smooth fabrics, in soft pencil or dressmaker's chalk pencil. If fabrics are transparent, full-sized patterns can be direct-traced from the page, using a finely sharpened HB pencil, or a coloured embroidery pencil. Another useful marking device is a pen which has air-soluble ink in it.

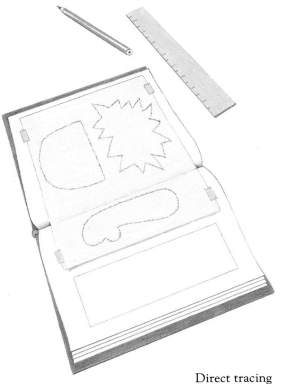

Direct tracing from the page.

After tracing a pattern the line remains on the fabric for a short time before it disappears.

### Diagram patterns

Copy these on to squared graph paper, using a ruler and a sharp HB pencil.

The lines on the paper will help you to keep corners square and accurate. You may find a flexible plastic ruler an aid when drawing curves. The ruler can be easily bent into a curve and then you simply pencil along its edge. The pattern shapes can either be cut directly from the graph paper or, if you wish to keep the pattern for repeated use, trace it on to tracing paper.

Enlarging a graph pattern.

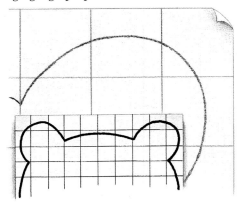

### Graph patterns

These patterns are given reduced in size on a squared grid. A scale is given and, to produce a full-sized pattern, you need squared dressmaker's paper marked with squares of the same scale. This paper is sold in large sheets, several to a packet, and can be obtained from dressmaking notions counters in shops and department stores.

To reproduce a graph pattern you copy the lines on your pattern paper, square for square.

### Transferring patterns

Patterns are transferred to the fabric with dressmaker's carbon paper. This is sold in sheets in packets of three or four colours, red, blue, yellow and white. A sheet is slipped between the pattern and fabric, and then the lines traced over with a tracing tool or a sharply-pointed HB pencil.

## Cutting sewing patterns

Trace the pattern from the book using tracing paper and a felt pen. Add any notations such as *fold, cut 2*. The patterns in this book include a seam allowance of $\frac{1}{2}$in (1.25cm). If, however, seam allowances are not included, remember to add them to all sides of a pattern piece. Cut out the pattern pieces and lay them on the fabric, matching grainlines or fold as appropriate.

The simplest patterns are made by drawing around existing objects. Household objects such as plates, cups and bowls make excellent templates.

## Layout

Whenever possible, fold the fabric in half and cut through two layers at once. This not only saves time, it ensures corresponding right and left pieces are accurately cut. Always fold fabric right

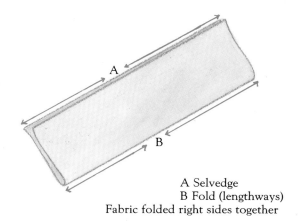

A Selvedge
B Fold (lengthways)
Fabric folded right sides together

sides together so that any markings are made on the wrong side.

Generally, fabric is folded lengthways. This means the fabric is folded so that the selvedges are together. If the instruction is to fold crossways, fold the fabric end to end, again right sides together.

If it is inappropriate to fold the fabric, or the instructions say to cut from a single layer, lay the pattern piece on the right side of the fabric. A pattern piece that needs two pieces cut should then be flipped over, face down, for the second piece in order to get a left and right piece.

## Fabric grain

Following the grain line is extremely important when laying patterns and cutting out fabric. The grain line generally referred to is parallel to the selvedge – along the engthways threads. The crossways grain is at right angles to the lengthways grain. If patterns are laid even slightly off-grain, the fabric pieces may ripple, pull or pucker when stitched, ruining the finished appearance.

## Seam allowance

All the patterns in this book include a seam allowance of $\frac{1}{2}$in (1.25cm). Most new sewing machines have measured grooves in the footplate so that the seam allowance can be accurately maintained. If your machine does not have this guide, stick a strip of masking tape to the footplate as a guideline.

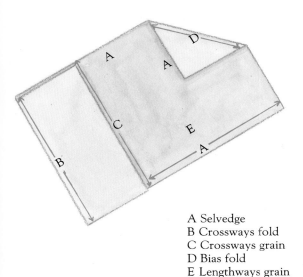

A Selvedge
B Crossways fold
C Crossways grain
D Bias fold
E Lengthways grain

## WOODWORK

While it is possible to make simple things in wood using the minimum of tools, one or two mechanical aids will make your work easier.

### Jig saw (fretsaw)

This tool is available with a variety of detachable blades, each for the type of wood you are cutting.

### Finishing sander

A finishing sander will save you hours of work. They come with different grades of sand paper and a beautiful finish to work is easily achieved.

### Try-square

This has a wooden or plastic stock and a metal blade at right angles. This essential piece of equipment is needed to ensure that all joints and edges are cut at right angles. It will also be used to check that pieces will fit well together.

**Using a try-square** Before starting any woodwork project you should mark the face side and the face edge of the wood. This is the surface that will show when the work is finished. When taking any check with the try-square, its wooden handle should always be laid against the face side of the wood.

### Tenon saw

This is used for cutting wood and will probably be the most useful tool in your toolbox. It has a rigid blade with pointed teeth. Choose either a 10 or 12in (25 or 30cm) saw with 14 to 16 teeth.

**Using a tenon saw** When you are using

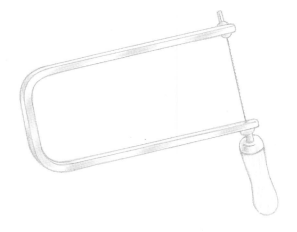

Jig saws (fretsaws) come with a variety of blades.

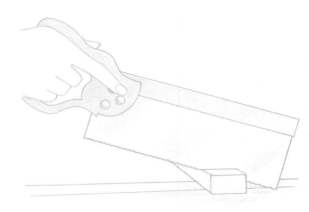

Working with a tenon saw.

a tenon saw for cutting wood, mark the cutting line on the face side of the wood, then lay the try-square along the face side to mark the cutting line, first on one edge and then on the other. Finally, mark the back of the wood and shade off the waste part which is to be cut away.

Cuts are always made on the waste side of the marked lines. This makes sure that the thickness of the saw will not cut away part of the shape you are making. Start the cut by placing your left thumb against the saw blade and make a light cut to begin, then start sawing along the whole length of the saw blade. If the blade will not move smoothly try stroking a scrap of wax candle along the teeth. Keep the saw upright while working. When the end of the cut is reached saw very lightly to avoid the wood breaking off and

An extra fine finish can be given to wood if, when you have finished the final sanding, the work is wetted with clean water. Leave it to dry and the grain will have raised. A final sanding with a fine grade paper will give a silky smoothness, ideal for painting or varnishing.

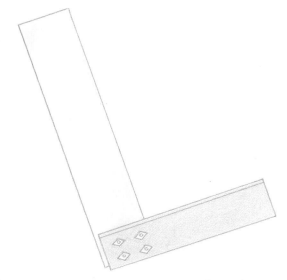

A try-square is vital for checking right-angles.

splintering underneath. Then check against the marked lines to make sure that you have cut the wood at the right angles. The edge of the wood can be lightly planed if necessary so that the cut is where you intended.

## Cordless screw driver

This is a great asset to a woodworker. It will drive screws into wood effortlessly and accurately.

**Using the screwdriver** Drill a shallow pilot hole which is the same diameter as the straight part of the screw (just beyond the head). This will make sure that the screw goes straight into the wood.

## Work bench and clamp

A strong table or work bench is essential for wood work and, wherever possible, work should be clamped to the bench. Use a piece of scrap wood under the metal pad of the clamp so that it does not crush and mark the work.

## Other items of equipment

To make simple toys and accessories, you will probably need the following items: a drill and bits, including countersinking bits, wood glue, glass and sandpaper in various grades, screws and nails and a hammer.

## Painting wood

Wood should be very smooth before painting and this may take several sandings, finishing with the very finest grade. Nails should be punched below the surface and any holes or blemishes filled with wood filler.

If you are making a toy, take great care that only non-toxic paint is used. Always take the advice of the supplier. Tiny tins of gloss or matt craft paints, available in a wide range of colours, are ideal for painting small toys. There is also a kind of craft paint that is diluted with water. This type of paint is used when you want the wood grain to show.

## Getting a good finish

Getting a really good painted finish takes time and preparation. Prime the wood with primer, then apply two thin coats of a suitable undercoat. Diluted emulsion paint makes a good undercoat. Rub the dry undercoat smooth again if bits of paint have stuck to the surface.

Before applying the final gloss coat, choose a fairly warm day if possible and do not wear anything woolly! Close the windows if there is a breeze which might bring hairs and dust into contact with your work.

Dip the bristles of the brush into the paint and draw the brush against the side of the tin to remove excess paint and any drips. Apply the paint lightly and immediately begin to brush out. This means spreading the paint in all directions from where you applied it. You will be surprised how far one brush-load of paint will go! Try to achieve a really thin coat of paint over the surface. Finally, brush out with all the strokes going in one direction lifting the brush into the air at the end of a stroke. In a few minutes, the surface will have smoothed itself out. Leave to dry, under cover if possible.

## POT POURRI

Pot pourri captures the fragrance of dried flowers, herbs, aromatic seeds and foliage. Once you have mastered a few basic techniques, it is easy to create your own different pot pourri mixtures.

### Drying flowers

Nearly any flower, herb, grass, seed or foliage is suitable for use in pot pourri.

Choose healthy pieces and try to gather them on a dry day. Discard bruised or damaged materials.

Spread the flower heads on sheets of newspaper and leave them in a warm, airy place to dry completely.

Whole rosebuds can be gathered and left to dry separately or you can hang them upside down in bunches of five roses with leaves intact in a warm airy place to dry. Herbs and lavender can be cut and hung upside down from the ceiling in small bunches to dry.

Check after about a week to see if the material is dry enough to use. It should feel papery and firm, not limp or damp.

Dried rose petals are an important ingredient in many pot pourri recipes. They keep their colour well.

Store prepared material in an airtight container such as a used ice cream carton with a lid. Keep flower groups separate, roses in one, lavender in another and so on. They will keep well like this in a cool place until you are ready to use them.

The dried material will have a natural fragrance but this will soon fade if you do not use a fixative. Orris root is one of the best, but you can also use spices from the store cupboard such as cinnamon, mixed spice, cloves, nutmeg, sea salt, lemon and orange peel.

### Essential oils

These are another vital fixative which will add depth and intensity of fragrance to pot pourri mixtures.

Essential oils are made by distilling different kinds of plant material.

All essential oils must be used very carefully. They should not be taken internally, be used directly on the skin or used as aromatherapy oils.

They are purely an added ingredient for pot pourri and other scented projects.

Keep them away from varnished wood and other fine surfaces, as drops of oil will stain.

Keep oils away from naked flame and avoid contact with hands, as the oil has a very strong perfume.

Never store the oils in plastic bottles but keep them in the glass bottles in which they were purchased.

Always use a dropper when adding oil. Store oil in a cool place with the cap tightly fixed, out of sight and reach of children and animals.

Use it sparingly, one drop at a time, as too much will upset the delicate balance of pot pourri fragrance.

### How to make pot pourri

Part of the fun of making pot pourri is in inventing your own mixtures, adding different herbs or flowers or mixing oils and spices to produce an individual fragrance.

Look for texture and colour as well as fragrance. Try to save a few whole flowers to scatter on top of pot pourri when you have made it.

Combine all the ingredients in a large

Roses, herbs and lavender hung to dry.

wooden or glass bowl. Then add the fixatives, orris root powder, herbs, spices, salt, to 'hold' the perfume and finally add the drops of essential oil. Stir the mixture to spread the contents.

Store pot pourri in an airtight container for four to six weeks. This length of time will ensure that it has matured and will hold its perfume. If the mint leaves are too large to look attractive in the finished pot pourri, tear them into smaller pieces.

## POT POURRI RECIPES:

### Lavender time

A traditional recipe suitable for
   perfuming linen.
4 cups of lavender flowers
2 cups of lemon mint leaves
1 cup of dried thyme
½ cup of coarse salt
1 tablespoon of powdered cloves
1 tablespoon of dried lemon peel
2 or 3 drops of lavender oil

### Wild flower pot pourri

This evocative mixture works well in
   wedding gift projects.
3 cups of pink rose petals
3 cups of clove variety carnation petals
2 cups of camomile flowers
1 cup of lavender flowers
1 cup of lemon verbena leaves
2 teaspoons of orris root powder
1 teaspoon of powdered cloves
2 or 3 drops of carnation oil

### Country breeze

A pretty pot pourri you can use to fill a
   sachet for a sleep pillow.
3 cups of red rose petals
2 cups of pink clover flowers
2 cups of apple mint leaves
1 cup of marjoram and sage leaves, mixed
1 cup of rose geranium leaves
1 cup of pink statice flowers
1 tablespoon of grated lemon peel
2 tablespoons of orris root powder
2 or 3 drops of rose geranium oil

### Rose dream

An original perfume. Use it for scenting
   drawer liners and writing paper.
5 cups of strong scented rose petals
4 bay leaves finely chopped
2 vanilla pods finely chopped
1 tablespoon of ground nutmeg
1 tablespoon of cinnamon powder
1 tablespoon of orris root powder

**Pine walk**

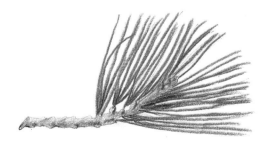

This invigorating pine fragrance can be
  used to perfume a coat hanger or a
  pillow.
3 cups of well-dried pine shavings
2 cups of shredded bay leaves
2 cups of shredded lemon balm leaves
1 cup of golden rod flowers
1 cup of peppermint leaves
2 teaspoons of mixed spice
2 teaspoons of orris root powder
2 or 3 drops of pine oil

### Flowers suitable for pot pourri
Chamomile, geranium, golden rod,
heather, lavender, lemon balm, marigold,
pansy, rose, salvia, strawflower, tansy,
yarrow.

### Herbs to discourage insects
Basil, bay, elder, meadowsweet, mint,
pennyroyal, rosemary, rue,
southernwood, wormwood.

## DRIED FLOWERS
### Wires and wiring
Wires can be purchased from florist's
shops, usually in small bundles.

For the projects in this book, three
sorts of wire have been used. They are
standard wire gauge nos. 22 and 20 (12in,
30cm long) and fine silver wire.

Attaching wires to flowers and other
material makes it easier to arrange them.
Take a flower in one hand and carefully
bind the wire three times round the stem.

### Binding with stem tape
Wired flower stems need to be covered
with stem tape (or gutta percha), which is

available in various shades from florist's
shops.

Hold the wired flower in one hand
and, starting at the top of the wire, twist
and firmly pull the stem tape round it
until the wire is covered.

### Wiring fir cones
Take one end of a 12in (30cm) no. 20
wire. Push it between the lowest seeds of
the fir cone, leaving about 1½in (4cm) of
wire protruding. Tightly wind the long
end of the wire in and out of the seeds
until both ends of the wire meet. Twist
the two wire ends together to secure
them. Trim them, cover them with stem
tape and bend them under the base of the
cone.

### Silk flowers
Silk flowers are widely obtainable and
useful for scented projects. They are also
easy to handle and individual pieces can
be snipped off the main stem with sharp
scissors. They can then be wired or sewn
in to an arrangement. They can be gently
wiped with a damp cloth to remove dust,
or carefully handwashed in luke warm
water and left to dry away from heat
sources.

It is worth while taking time to select
natural-looking material.

### Pressing flowers
Many different types of flowers, herbs
and foliage are suitable for pressing but
avoid fleshy specimens, as they do not
press well.

You can use a flower press or, easier
still, place items between sheets of
blotting paper and press in a heavy book.

Gather material on a dry day, choosing
only perfect pieces. Spread them on
sheets of blotting paper so that they do
not touch each other.

Place them under a pile of heavy books
and leave them for about four to six
weeks to dry. Some materials such as
petals, leaves and grasses, dry faster than
others, so check regularly. The material
will change to muted shades when dry.

Experiment with different kinds of

flowers and grasses until you have built up a collection ready for use.

Once pressed, remove the blotting paper with tweezers and store flat between clean sheets of paper.

Some flowers suitable for pressing are buttercup, daisy, freesia, pansy, primula, rose, violet, foliage and grasses.

### Florist's foam

Two kinds of foam are used in floral arrangements, brown, which is dry and used for dried flower arrangements, (available in blocks, balls, cones and cylinders) and green, sold in blocks and used for wet arrangements. This must be soaked in water before use.

## MAKING BOWS
### Ribbon bows for wiring

To make ribbon bows as a final touch to a gift, form a length of ribbon in a figure of eight, holding the centre between thumb and forefinger. With the same length of ribbon, make another figure of eight. Hold the bows together at the centre and bind them together with lightweight wire, leaving two wire 'legs'

If you find this is too difficult, use several single loops on top of each other.

### Sewn ribbon bows

Cut a length of ribbon in two, with one piece slightly shorter than the other. Fold the ends of the longer piece in to the middle, overlapping slightly. Sew a gathering thread across the centre and tie tightly. Fold the shorter piece in half round the waist of the bow. Sew in place at the back to form the knot. Arrange the ends neatly and trim.

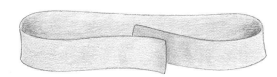

Fold the ends to the middle.

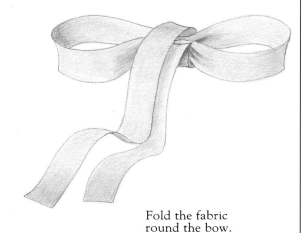

Fold the fabric round the bow.

Sew across the centre.

Gather up tightly and tie off.

Ribbons.

### Fabric bows

Use a strip of fabric twice as wide as the ribbon required plus ½in (13mm). Fold the strip in half lengthways with right sides facing and stitch along the length, taking a ¼in (6mm) seam, leaving the ends open. Press the seam open. Turn right side out and press the strip so that the seam is at the back. Form the bow in the same way as for sewn ribbon bows and finish by tucking in the raw edges. Oversew the ends.

### Decorative trimmings

Ribbons and braids come in most widths and colours. As well as plain ribbons in satin, grosgrain, velvet or taffeta there are printed ribbons and many decoratively-edged ribbons.

Sew narrow ribbons and braids with one line of central stitching. Machine-stitch wider ribbons down both edges, always stitching in the same direction to prevent puckering.

Lace also comes in a variety of patterns and widths. Choose cotton lace if the item is to be ironed.

Pretty broderie anglaise is available flat with slots for ribbon insertion, and pre-gathered.

Beaded trimming is also obtainable.

## STENCILLING

You can create your own stencil designs freehand or copy or trace an illustration from a book or picture. When you have chosen a design, draw it on to tracing paper, then transfer it to card or a piece of acetate.

To cut the stencil you will need either very sharp, short pointed scissors or a craft knife.

Always cut stencils on a firm, protected surface and be extra careful when handling sharp tools, keeping fingers well out of the way.

Mark the card or acetate sheet with a fine waterproof felt-tipped pen.

If you plan to use more than one colour, you will need separate stencils for each colour.

Acrylic paints are suitable for most projects, fabric paints are suitable for fabrics and you can make a quick stencil on paper with felt-tipped pens.

Short, stubby brushes especially for stencilling can be purchased from art shops but almost any brush can be used on small projects.

Clear and spray varnish can be used to protect a design.

Painting a stencil.

Cutting a stencil.

# SEWING AND EMBROIDERY EQUIPMENT

Most households already have the basic tools required to begin sewing. However, it is a good idea to overhaul the sewing basket and ensure the equipment is in good useable condition.

## Dressmaking shears

A good, sharp pair of dressmaking shears should only be used to cut fabric – not paper (and never use them in the kitchen!). They should have sharp blades with pointed tips, and shaped handles which will make cutting easier.

## Embroidery scissors

A small pair of pointed embroidery scissors is extremely handy for trimming small areas, clipping seams and thread. The small size makes handling difficult areas much easier, with a greater control on the amount snipped or cut. Use them to avoid accidentally cutting through seams or clipping away more than is intended.

## Paper scissors

A spare pair of scissors, that can be used for cutting out paper, patterns etc. Preferably choose a large pair so that cutting out big pattern pieces does not become tedious. Always cut out patterns accurately along the cutting line, as an extra ½in (1.25cm) multiplied by 2–3 seams could alter the overall fit.

## Quick clips

A small scissor with short blades and thumb control that is very useful for clipping small areas, tailor's tacks and thread ends.

## Pinking shears

Very useful for cutting out craft fabrics, felt and card.

## Rotary cutter

Ideal for cutting out patterns as the blade can be used alongside a straight edge, such as a ruler.

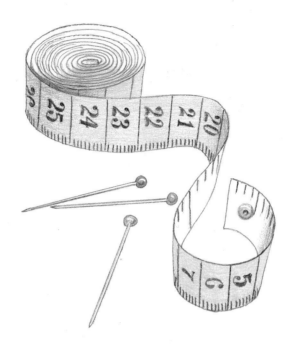

A good tape measure and sharp pins are essential.

## Scissor tuner

And finally, just in case you accidentally cut through a pin or otherwise damage your scissor blades, a scissor tuner is very handy. By running the faulty blade through the tuner, you can get rid of any burrs or snags that could catch on the fabric and cause unsightly pulls and tears.

## Pins

There are many different types and lengths of pin, designed for various uses. For general use the glass/plastic-headed pins are preferable as they are easy to remove as you sew. They are also more easily found if accidently dropped! As with needles, pins will become blunt after repeated use so they should be replaced regularly.

Generally, it is advisable to pin at right angles to the seam so that the pins can be removed as you sew. However, when sewing fabric that marks very easily, such as suede, only pin within the seam allowance. It is also advisable to remove

| Needle Chart | | |
|---|---|---|
| Fabric Type | Hand | Machine |
| **Very light fabric:** chiffon, silk, lace | 9,10,11,12 | 9,11 (70,80) |
| **Light fabric:** silks, lawn, taffeta, voile | 8 | 11 (80) |
| **Medium light fabric:** gingham, cotton, satin, wool crêpe | 7,8 | 11,14 (80,90) |
| **Medium fabric:** flannel, velvet, pique, corduroy, linen | 6,7 | 14 (90) |
| **Medium heavy fabric:** towelling, denim, tweed, felt, fleece, chintz, fake fur | 6 | 14,16 (90,100) |
| **Heavy fabric:** wax-covered, ticking, corduroy, canvas, upholstery, fabrics, leather, suede | 1,2,3 | 16,18 (100,110) |

pins before pressing, otherwise you may press in a pin indentation that refuses to fade later.

## Needles

Both sewing machine needles and hand sewing needles will become blunt after repeated use and should be replaced regularly. Needles are available in different sizes for different fabric thicknesses. Very fine point needles are used to sew fine fabrics, sheers and silks while a larger, heavier needle is used for coarser fabric. For sewing machines the choice is further extended to different *types* of needle for different fabric qualities. Ball-point needles are used for knitted/jersey fabrics – the rounded tip pushes the fibres apart rather than piercing them and thus prevents snags or runs. A jeans needle is extra tough for thick heavy fabric while a twin needle can stitch two rows at the same time.

## Darning needle or bodkin

These are very useful for threading ribbon or elastic through casings.

## Measuring aids

A good tape measure is essential for measuring fabric accurately. As a cloth tape measure can stretch with age and measurements may thus be inaccurate, a plastic-coated retractable measure is preferable, with both inches and centimetres to enable the choice of imperial or metric measurements.

A long ruler is also a good idea for drawing out diagrams and patterns and as a straight edge when marking out on fabric. Wooden yard sticks are available and are equally useful, particularly with hemming.

## Tracing paper

Tracing paper is usually recommended for tracing same-size patterns or motifs but ordinary kitchen grease-proof paper will do just as well. Simply trace from the book and then transfer to the fabric, including any markings.

### Dressmaker's carbon paper

Available in packs, dressmaker's carbon is used with tracing paper to transfer patterns to fabric. Place the paper carbon side down on the wrong side of the fabric and lay the traced pattern in position. Run a tracing wheel along the cutting lines to pick out the pattern. The carbon paper can be re-used many times.

### Graph paper

When patterns are scaled down, they need to be transferred to graph paper in order to enlarge them to the correct size. Dressmaker's graph paper is available in various scales, thus it is necessary to use the paper that corresponds to the scale quoted on the drawing.

### Chalk pencils/tailor's chalk

Tailor's chalk is used to mark placement lines, darts, pockets, points and other pattern markings on the fabric. A chalk pencil can be used to draw patterns directly on to the fabric. They are especially useful when no paper pattern is required – such as simple squares, rectangles or circles drawn round plates. Both chalk types should brush off easily; however, it is still advisable to make any markings on the wrong side of the fabric.

### Quick unpick

A quick unpick is an extremely useful tool for quickly unpicking incorrect seams, saving a lot of time and

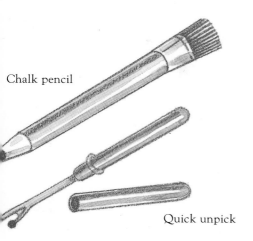

Chalk pencil

Quick unpick

frustration. To use, insert the longer edge point into the seam, with the beaded edge laid against the fabric. Push along gently, so that stitches will be cut by the sharp curve of metal at the end.

A quick unpick is also a great tool for slashing buttonholes. Place a pin at one end of the buttonhole to be slashed and then holding the fabric firmly in one hand, push the long edge of the quick unpick through at the other end of the buttonhole. With the beaded end resting on the stitching, push the quick unpick along until it reaches the pin.

### Thread

The variety of thread types and colours now available can be overwhelming. As a general rule, however, use a thread made from the same fibres as the fabric – cotton with cotton, polyester with man-made, silk with silk. When in doubt, or when mixing fabric types, an all-round, very good general purpose thread is a polyester-covered cotton which has the give of cotton and durability of polyester.

To gauge the actual shade of the thread and ensure a perfect match, unreel a little and match with the fabric (in natural light). If the exact shade is not available, choose one that is slightly darker than the fabric.

### Top-stitching thread

Top-stitching thread is thicker than ordinary threads and is ideal for machine-embroidery. However, top-stitching can be done just as effectively using ordinary thread.

### Embroidery threads

Hand-embroided motifs, faces and highlights look better if stitched in embroidery threads. Available in skeins, there is a tremendous choice of colour and sheen. Although many skeins have six-strands these are generally split and used in two or three-strand thicknessess. In this book facial features have been embroidered and decorative detail added using three strands of embroidery thread.

177

Other haberdashery items that are useful and time-saving include:

### Point turner
A hard, usually plastic, ruler with a firm point. By pushing the point-turner into corners and angles, you can ensure a crisp, even point. Avoid using knitting needles or scissor points as there is a risk of pushing them through the stitching.

### Fade-away pens
These are useful for marking stitching lines, darts, pleats or pocket placements. Even though the markings should fade, it is advisable to work on the wrong side of the fabric.

### Turning loop
A thin metal rod with a catch hook on one end, a turning loop is ideal for turning through thin straps or ties. The hook is passed along the stitched tie to the end and hooked around the seam allowance before pulling back, turning the fabric to the right side.

### Fastenings
There are many ways of fastening two pieces of fabric – from zips, buttons and poppers to lace and ribbons. The main fasteners used for the projects in this book are poppers, buttons and Velcro. The type of fastening to be used depends on the use of the item.

### Closure tape – Velcro
Velcro consists of two strips, one with tiny hooks and one with a pile. When pressed together these intermesh and hold the two sides together.

### Snaps/poppers
These are widely available in black, nickel or clear plastic in a range of sizes and weights.

### Buttons
When attaching buttons, use three or four stitches with doubled thread or buttonhole twist thread. In addition, always wind the thread around the stitching between button and fabric two or three times which will then make it easier to fasten the button.

Buttonholes should be slightly longer than the button. Always interface fabric in which buttonholes are to be made for greater stability, before stitching the buttonhole. Without it, the close stitching can pucker and jam in the sewing machine.

### Zip fasteners
Zips are the most common form of fastening on garments. Different weights, lengths and colours are available – the choice of which will depend on the item made. Generally, a lightweight fabric requires a lightweight, polyester zip. Heavier garments need stronger metal zips. The zip length should be $\frac{1}{2}$–1in (1.25–2.5cm) longer than the opening.

It is advisable to use a zipper foot when inserting zips in order to stitch close to the teeth. Always baste the zip in position and check for fit before machine-stitching in place.

### Fabrics
Before you start any project, look through your scraps of fabric. You will probably find a remnant that you can use. When you are buying fabric for a dress or making a home-sewing project, it is a good idea to buy an extra half metre. This, together with any off-cuts, can often be put to good purpose, such as a set of matching accessories for a dressing table or some colourful items for the kitchen.

When selecting fabrics, remember that closely woven fabrics tend to fray less than loosely woven types. These fabrics are also easier to sew and generally give a good result. Make sure they have easy-care properties, so that they can be washed without the colours running and need little ironing.

Colours will be a personal choice, but when looking at a printed fabric, bear in mind the finished size of the project and avoid using large prints on small items. Most of the projects in this book will look best if they are made up in small sprig fabrics. The scale of checked and striped fabrics must be also noted; go for the small check ginghams rather than the larger versions whenever possible.

## Interfacing

An interfacing is an extra layer added to the wrong side of the fabric. It is used to add body and to help with the drape. It can be another type of fabric that is compatible with the main fabric or it can be a branded interfacing. These are available in a variety of weights, either sew-in or iron-on and suitable for woven or knitted fabrics. The choice will depend on the effect required. As a general rule, however, the interfacing should be of a similar weight to the fabric and should also have the same laundering requirements.

When using iron-on interfacing, use a damp cloth and hot iron, pressing each area for approximately 10 seconds. Lift the iron, move to the next area and press again – do not push the iron along as it may stretch the interfacing or fabric which, in turn, will cause puckering. Always allow the fabric to dry and cool completely before continuing with the project. If handled too quickly, the interfacing may come unstuck.

## Stuffing/filling

Polyester stuffing is preferable, particularly for toys, as it is washable. Do not be afraid of stuffing firmly, pushing into the corners and curves with a point turner or pencil. If inadequately stuffed, the item will very quickly lose its shape, so shape as you go, adjusting the stuffing accordingly.

## Wadding (batting)

Wadding is the layer of fabric that is sandwiched between two other fabrics in quilting. Washable, polyester wadding comes in a range of different weights from light to an extra heavyweight (only used in upholstery). Use a lightweight wadding to give fabric extra body, and the medium and heavyweight versions for quilting, or when an extra layer for warmth is required.

## Decorative trimmings

Small projects often look prettier with the addition of a decorative trim. Ribbons and braids come in most widths and the colour ranges are extensive so it is usually easy to find a good match. Besides plain ribbons in polyester satin, grosgrain, velvet and taffeta, there are printed ribbons, jacquard weaves and a variety of decoratively edged ribbons to be found. Attach narrow ribbons and braids by stitching them down the centre. With wider ribbons, machine-stitch down both edges, always stitching in the same direction to prevent puckering.

## Sewing machine

Although a sewing machine is not essential it certainly speeds up sewing! Basic requirements include straight-stitch, zigzag, satin stitch and easy buttonholes, a choice of feet including a zipper foot and a choice of stitching speeds. Sewing machines range from basic models to high-tech computerized machines with endless stitch combinations. Bear in mind these when buying a machine:

1  Choose one that has the features you need now and some you might want in the future.
2  Look for good basic features: choice of automatic stitches, stitch speed regulator, simple buttonholes, easy foot control, variable needle position, good operator manual or video.
3  Try out the machine in the shop, testing on your own fabrics.
4.  Ensure that there is a good after sales service.

## STITCHES

Darts, pocket placements and pleats need to be transferred from the pattern to the fabric. The traditional method uses tailor's tacks. These are large-looped stitches made at the placement points through both layers of the fabric before the pattern is removed.

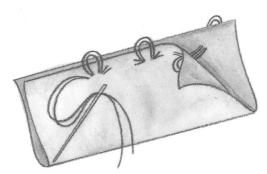

Tailor's tacks – large-looped stitches

Use a contrasting thread and make 3–4 large, loose stitches. Cut the threads carefully, remove the pattern and then gently pull the two fabric layers apart, cutting the threads between the layers as you go. Both layers will then have corresponding markings. Alternatively, use a chalk pencil, fade-away pen or dressmaker's carbon paper, again marking both fabric layers.

### Basting/tacking

When joining two pieces of fabric it is sometimes advisable to baste (tack) them together first. While straight seams can be pinned and machine-stitched without basting, trickier curved areas should be basted together. This will ensure that both layers are fed through the machine-stitched at the same pace, avoiding one layer creeping or stretching.

To baste (tack), knot one end of the thread and with a running-stitch, make $\frac{1}{2}$in (1.25cm) long stitches along the stitching line. Use a contrasting thread that is clearly visible later. To remove, clip the knot and pull through. On long seams, it is advisable to clip and remove the basting thread at intervals. Different stitching techniques can be used

to make seams, attach motifs or as a decorative finish. The following are a few of the most common stitches and those used throughout this book.

### Machine stitches
### Straight stitch

The most common and standard stitch used to sew seams. First pin the fabric layers, right sides together, placing the pins at right angles to the fabric for easy removal. Then stitch, back-stitching at the begining and end of each seam. The

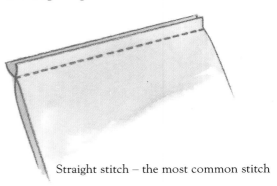

Straight stitch – the most common stitch

stitches should be even in size and tension. If puckering occurs, increase the stitch length slightly. Always test on a scrap of fabric first.

### Zigzag stitch

This very versatile stitch is often used to neaten seam edges and as a decorative finish. Use a small zigzag stitch on lightweight fabrics and a larger stitch for the heavier fabrics. A zigzag stitch can also be used to sew seams on stretchy jersey. The finish will have more give and will be less likely to snap when stretched.

Zigzag stitch – a decorative finish

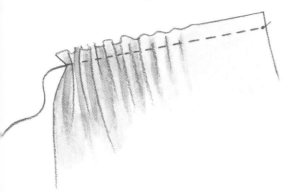

## Gathering stitch

Large, loose stitches are used to gather fabrics for ruffles and frills. For long stretches of gathering, break off the thread at intervals which will be easier to gather than one long row. To gather, pull up each of the threads, adjusting fullness as you go.

## Stay stitch

Curved areas and areas that require extra handling should be stay-stitched prior to joining pieces. This is to prevent unwanted stretching. Simply stitch in the seam allowance, approximately $\frac{1}{8}$in (3mm) from the edge using a normal size stitch.

## Satin stitch

A very close zigzag-stitch that looks like one continuous line. To make satin-stitch, adjust the width and length dials until the width is approx $\frac{1}{8}$in (3mm) and there is hardly any gap between stitches.

A ball-point needle is preferable as it will suit most fabrics. To achieve a smoother satin-stitch slightly loosen the upper tension.

## Top-stitching

Top-stitching is simply a term used to describe stitches on the top, outer side of a garment or item. Top-stitching can be in a contrasting or matching thread and it can be a simple straight stitch or a decorative stitch.

Always stitch with the right side uppermost, taking it slowly and carefully as, of course, the stitching will be visible. If two rows are stitched close together, try using a twin needle which stitches both lines at once. Use contrasting thread when you are confident of achieving a very straight even line of stitching. Finally, as top-stitching is purely decorative, it can be left out if preferred.

## Hand stitches
### Slipstitch

This is used to join 2 folded edges, such as a gap in a seam. Working from right to left, bring the needle out through the upper folded edge. Slip the needle through the lower folded edge for about $\frac{1}{4}$in (6mm). Pull the needle and thread through. Slip the needle through the upper folded edge for about $\frac{1}{4}$in (6mm). Pull through and continue through opposite folded edges.

### Hemming stitch

Used for hems or when finishing the underside of a bound seam, simply take up a single thread from the garment fabric and then bring the needle up diagonally through the edge of the binding or hem allowance.

### Blind stitch

Similar to hemming stitch and also often used to hem garments, a blind stitch is inconspicuous as it is hidden. This is achieved by rolling back the edge of the hem or facing about $\frac{1}{4}$in (6mm), picking up one thread from the hem, then picking up one thread from the garment diagonally below. Repeat from hem to garment, without pulling the stitches tight. Roll the edge down and press. No stitching should be visible.

BETTER TECHNIQUES

### Back-stitch

This is a strong stitch, useful for repairing seams and for hard-to-reach seams that can not be machined. On the right side the finished seam will look as if it is machine-stitched whilst the stitches on the underside will overlap and be twice as long.

With right sides together, bring the needle to the upperside along the seam line. Go back through to the underside approximately $\frac{1}{8}$in (3mm) behind the first point, bringing the needle to the upperside again $\frac{1}{8}$in (3mm) in front of the first point. Keep inserting the needle through the left side of the previous stitch and bringing it back up a stitch ahead.

### Running stitch

As a very basic and quick stitch the running stitch is used for easing and gathering. Several stitches can be worked in one go, running the needle in and out of the fabric before pulling the thread through. Use large stitches for gathering and smaller stitches for easing.

### Ease-stitch

Ease-stitch is formed by a running stitch and is used to stabilize and ease a fabric edge. It is used when a full or curved edge is to be joined to a straight edge. By ease-stitching the curved edge, you can ease the fullness into the straight edge.

### Overhand/whipstitch

Basically the same stitch, they hold two edges together – an overhand or a whipstitch is particularly useful for adding lace edgings or ribbon trims. Insert the needle from back to front, up over the top and back through again. An overhand stitch is inserted at a diagonal angle and whipstitch is inserted from back to front at right angles to the fabric.

### Embroidery stitches

There are literally hundreds of embroidery stitches to choose from when you are decorating fabrics. Here in the book are some of the most popular.

### Straight stitch

These are often used on dolls' faces to indicate eyelashes and sometimes for attaching felt eyes. The stitches are

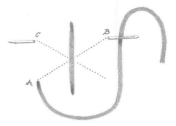

worked in a six-point star. Bring the needle through at A, insert it at B and bring it through again at C.

### Chain stitch

This is a simple yet effective decorative stitch. Bring the needle through at A and, with the thread below the needle, insert it beside A at B. The thread forms a loop.

Bring the needle through at C, pull through gently, ready to start the next chain-stitch. To work a detached chain-stitch, from C work a tying-stitch over the loop.

### French knots

A French knot is made by twisting the thread around the needle. First bring the needle through to the front of the work in the place that the knot is to be made.

Holding the thread taut, wrap it around the needle three times. Insert the needle back through the work close to the point where it emerged until the knot remains on the fabric surface.

## SEAMS AND SEAM FINISHES

In this book we have mainly used straight seams as the most common and easily created seams. A straight seam is formed by placing fabric layers, right sides together, matching raw edges and stitching along the stitching line – leaving ½in (1.25cm) seam allowance.

### French seam

A French seam is ideal for sheer fabrics as it encloses all raw edges giving a very neat finish to both sides of the fabric. On the outside it looks just like an ordinary straight seam, inside is a neat tuck.

Pin the *wrong* sides together, and then sew ¼in (6mm) from the raw edges. Trim the seam allowance to within ⅛in (3mm) and press. Fold back along the seam so that the *right* sides are together. Machine-stitch along the stitching line, which is now ¼in (6mm) from the seamed edge. Press again.

### Stretchy seams/sheer fabrics

When fabric has been cut on the bias or is a stretchy fabric, one of the fabric layers may tend to stretch when stitching. Similarly, very lightweight voile or sheer fabrics can pucker or jam in the machine. To prevent either problem arising, place a layer of tissue paper between the fabric and footplate. Stitch in the normal way, through both fabric and paper. Then tear the paper away.

### Bias cut edges

Again use tissue paper under the seam to prevent uneven stretching. In addition, slightly stretch the fabric as you stitch so that the finished edge will not pucker. Before hemming garments with bias seams, hang overnight to allow them to stretch to their natural level.

### Seam finishes

The seam allowance should be neatened or finished to give a neat appearance, to prevent fraying and to help support the garment shape. The type of seam finish desired will depend on the use of the item and weight of the fabric.

For lightweight fabrics both the seam allowances can be folded to one side and treated as one. Again, either turn the raw edges of both to the inside and stitch together, or zigzag stitch over the edges. Another finish for lightweight seams is the self-bound seam. Trim one seam allowance to a scant ⅛in (3mm) and then turn the raw edge of the remaining seam allowance under and machine-stitch over the trimmed seam.

For mediumweight fabrics, each seam allowance should be treated separately. First press the seam open, then either turn the raw edge under ⅛in (3mm) on both sides and machine stitch – working in the same direction in which seam was sewn, or zigzag stitch over the edge of either side.

For heavyweight fabrics, such as unlined jackets or coats a bound edge is ideally suited. Open out the seam allowances and press. Then encase each raw edge in double fold bias binding and machine-stitch in place.

Seam allowances that will be encased can be graded or layered to avoid bulk. Cut the lower seam allowance to a scant ⅛in (3mm) and the next one slightly larger.

## SPECIAL EFFECTS
### Appliqué

Appliqué is an attractive and simple way of adding motifs, colour and texture by attaching different fabrics to the base fabric. There are two popular ways in which to appliqué, the easier and quicker of these is the bonded method.

First cut the piece to be appliquéd according to the specific pattern. Add Bondaweb, a fusible adhesive with paper backing, to the wrong side of the appliqué. Peel the backing off and place on the right side of the main fabric, in the position required. If different pieces join together, overlap the edges by ⅛in (3mm) before pressing with a damp cloth to bond in place. Finish with a satin-stitch around the edges. Use a top thread that matches the appliqué and white bobbin thread.

183

Peel off the backing paper.

If the appliqué fabric or main fabric cannot be dampened and heavily pressed because of the texture, an alternative, dry method can be used. Cut a square around the appliqué, at least 1in (2.5cm) wider than the appliqué itself. With the right sides uppermost, pin in place. Using a small straight stitch, machine around the appliqué edge before trimming the excess fabric away from the appliqué square. Trim close to the stitching. Finish as before with a satin stitch border.

### Quilting

The textured look of the quilting is created by stitching two or more layers of fabric together in a set design or pattern. For added thickness and in order to produce the traditional raised effect, the layers can include one of wadding, flannel or foam. An easy alternative is to use a special iron-on Quiltex interfacing. The lines of adhesive provided can then be used as quilting guidelines.

For a very special effect, quilt round

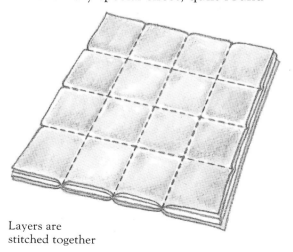

Layers are
stitched together

the fabric design or part of it to emphasize specific design features. The following tips will ensure trouble-free quilting:

● Experiment on a sample of the fabric layers to be quilted to check tension.
● Baste all layers together around the edges and, if it is a large area, across the centre. This will prevent the layers shifting unevenly.
● Mark quilting lines on the right side of the fabric with a chalk pencil unless using ready-printed interfacing. If the quilting is to follow the fabric design, use that as your stitching guide.
● Quilt garment sections before joining them together as large areas of quilting can reduce the overall size of the fabric piece.

### Ribbon weaving

A woven area of ribbon adds a decorative finish to cushions, pillow slips etc.

Weave the horizontal strips
in and out of the vertical
ones

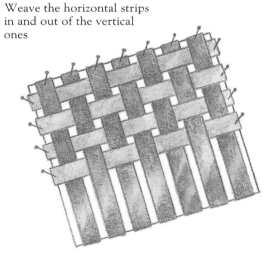

To weave ribbon first decide on the size of the area required and cut a piece of Bondaweb to that size. Cut the ribbon for the horizontal and vertical strands into equal lengths 1in (2.5cm) longer than the width and length of the piece to be woven. Anchor the Bondaweb to a padded surface or piece of card and then pin the top end of the vertical ribbon strips to the Bondaweb. Add the horizontal strips one at a time, weaving in and out of the vertical strips. Pin either side to hold in place. Once completed, press to bond and then turn the raw edges under and position the woven panel as required on the main fabric.

## FINISHING TOUCHES

**Piping:** Piping is a strip of bias-cut fabric, folded and set into a seam for a decorative finish. For a harder-wearing finish, such as on cushions, the piping covers cord.

Piping cord comes in several thicknesses for different applications. To estimate the width of the covering fabric measure round the cord and then add twice $\frac{5}{8}$in (15mm).

**Bias strips:** First, find the bias of the fabric. Fold over a corner of the fabric to meet the cut edge, the diagonal fold is the bias of the fabric. Cut through this fold. Use a rule and tailor's chalk to measure strips of the desired width from the diagonally cut edge.

Pin, baste and stitch strips together along the straight grain ends.

Place the cord centrally to the wrong side of the fabric and fold the strip round the cord. Baste closely against the cord. With a piping foot on the sewing machine, stitch down the strip close beside the cord.

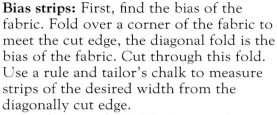

Fold over a corner to find the bias.

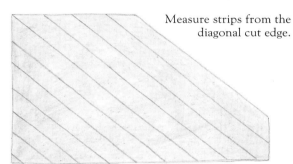
Measure strips from the diagonal cut edge.

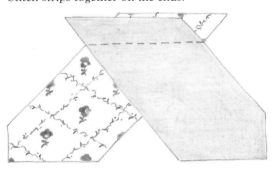
Stitch strips together on the ends.

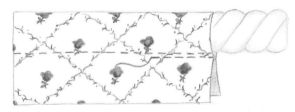
Stitch the fabric round the cord.

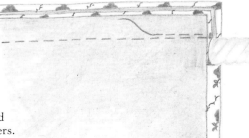
Stitch the covered cord between the fabric layers.

**Inserting piping:** Baste the prepared piping between two fabric layers, matching raw edges. Stitch on the seam line.

**Joining piping:** Start stitching ⅜in (9mm) from the end. When you come to the other end trim the cord to meet the first cord. Trim the fabric covering back to ½in (12.5mm). Butt the cords, dab a touch of fabric adhesive to the ends so that they stick together. Fold under the trimmed fabric edge ¼in (6mm). Wrap over the starting end of the piping. Continue stitching.

### Frills

**Single frill:** Decide on the finished width of the frill and add ½in (12.5mm) for a doubled hem and ⅝in (15mm) for the seam allowance. To estimate the length, measure along the place to be frilled and double the measurement. (If the fabric is very thick, only allow one and a half times the measurement.) Turn a double ¼in (6mm) hem along the bottom edge. Press and machine-stitch.

Work 2 rows of gathering-stitches along the top edge either side of the seamline. (If the frill is very long, divide the frill into equal sections and gather each section in turn.) Pull the gathers up evenly to fit the main fabric. Pin, then baste the frill to the main fabric, working across the gathering-stitches to hold the frill in place. Stitch the frill in place.

Remove basting threads. If the ends need to be neatened, work a double hem to match the bottom hem before gathering.

When making up a continuous frill, such as for a cushion, pin and stitch the frill-strip short ends together into a ring before gathering.

Turn and stitch a double hem on a single frill.

Work 2 rows of gathering along the top edge.

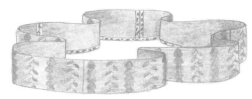

For a continuous frill, stitch short ends together.

### Fabric Width Conversion Chart

| 35"–36" | 44"–45" | 52"–54" | 58"–60" |
|---|---|---|---|
| 90cm | 115cm | 140cm | 150cm |
| 1¾(1.60m) | 1⅜(1.30m) | 1⅛(1.10m) | 1(1m) |
| 2(1.90m) | 1⅝(1.50m) | 1⅜(1.30m) | 1¼(1.20m) |
| 2¼(2.10m) | 1¾(1.60m) | 1½(1.40m) | 1⅜(1.30m) |
| 2½(2.30m) | 2⅛(2m) | 1¾(1.60m) | 1⅝(1.50m) |
| 2⅞(2.70m) | 2¼(2.10m) | 1⅞(1.80m) | 1¾(1.60m) |
| 3⅛(2.90m) | 2½(2.30m) | 2(1.90m) | 1⅞(1.80m) |
| 3⅜(3.10m) | 2¾(2.60m) | 2¼(2.10m) | 2(1.90m) |
| 3¾(3.50m) | 2⅞(2.70m) | 2⅜(2.20m) | 2¼(2.10m) |
| 4¼(3.90m) | 3⅛(2.90m) | 2⅝(2.40m) | 2⅜(2.20m) |
| 4½(4.20m) | 3⅜(3.10m) | 2¾(2.60m) | 2⅝(2.40m) |

**Double frill:** For a double frill, you need twice the required width and twice the seam allowance. Fold the strip lengthways, wrong sides facing, and baste

Baste and gather both layers together.

the raw edges together. Then gather and apply the frill as for the single frill, working both layers together. If you need to neaten the ends, fold the frill ends right sides facing and stitch across the ends. Trim the seam allowance and turn the frill right side out. Then gather and apply as for the single frill.

**Binding edges**

Bias binding is a neat way of finishing a raw edge as well as adding a touch of colour or pattern. Bias binding can be purchased ready-made in plain-coloured or patterned cotton or in acetate satin. If you wish to make your own bias binding, cut bias strips (see page 108). Press the sides of the strips to the centre by one quarter.

To bind the edge of a piece of fabric, unfold one edge of the binding and lay against the fabric with right sides facing. The crease of the fold lies along the seamline. Pin, baste and stitch in the crease. Trim the fabric edge a little and fold the binding over the edge to the wrong side. Baste, then slipstitch in place, working over the previous stitches.

If the binding is to be top-stitched, work the first stage of application in the same way. Bring the binding over the raw edge then baste and machine-stitch in place.

**Sewing tip**

When instructions indicate that the seam allowance is to be added, first re-fold the fabric, right sides facing. Pin out the pattern. Draw round the outline of the pattern pieces using pencil or dressmaker's chalk pencil. (Add all marks etc.) Cut out $\frac{3}{8}$in (9mm) from the pattern edge. Unpin the pattern. Baste the fabric pieces together, and stitch along the chalked line. This method enables you to achieve accurate stitching and perfect straight seams.

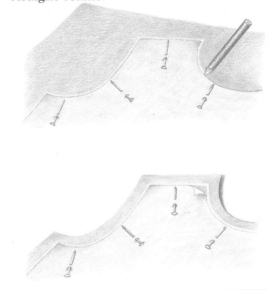

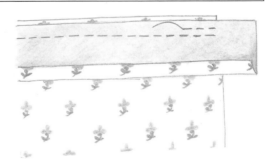

Open the binding and baste, then stitch along the fold line.

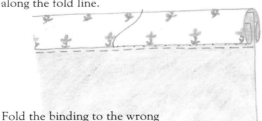

Fold the binding to the wrong side and slipstitch in place.

### Mitred corners

**Mitring a turned-in edge:** On a single hem, press under $\frac{1}{4}$in (6mm). Turn up the hem to the required length and press.

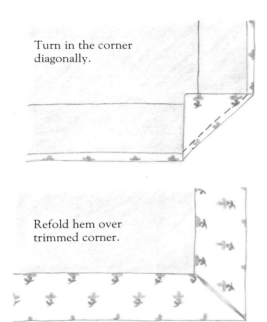

Turn in the corner diagonally.

Refold hem over trimmed corner.

Unfold and turn in the corner diagonally so that the diagonal fold meets the hem fold and press. Trim off the corner, leaving $\frac{1}{4}$in (6mm). Refold the hem over the trimmed corner.

**Mitring a flat trimming:** Place the trim against the fabric edge; pin and stitch in place up to the corner and fasten off. Fold the trimming back on itself, with the fold matching the next edge; pin firmly. Turn down the trimming along the next edge, pressing the diagonal fold that forms across the corner. Lift the trimming and stitch across the diagonal crease. Trim off excess and replace trimming. Continue stitching along the next edge. When all the corners have been mitred in the same way, stitch round the trimming along the inside edge.

**Mitre binding:** Unfold the edge of the binding and place against the edge, as explained before. Pin and stitch in the crease of the binding up to the seam line of the next edge, fasten off threads securely. Fold the binding diagonally away from the fabric, aligning the binding edge with the edge of the next side. Pin and stitch again, beginning the stitching from the seamline. Take the binding over the raw edge to the opposite side, folding the excess fabric into a neat mitre. On the wrong side, tuck under the excess binding to form a neat mitre as well. Pin and slipstitch the remaining folded edge of binding in place, stitching across the mitre on each side, only when the binding is wide.

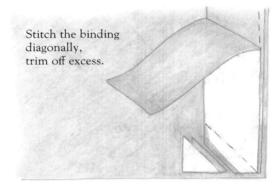

Stitch the binding diagonally, trim off excess.

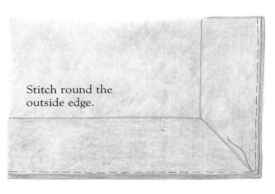

Stitch round the outside edge.

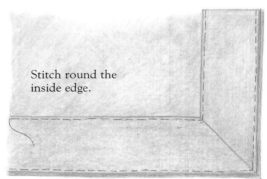

Stitch round the inside edge.

# Index

# GLOSSARY OF TERMS

| UK | US | UK | US |
|---|---|---|---|
| adhesive | glue | muslin | cheesecloth or gauze |
| Bondaweb | fusible webbing | | |
| broderie anglaise | eyelet lace | neaten | finish |
| card (material) | cardboard | oddments | scraps |
| concertina | accordion | oversew | overcast |
| cotton bud | cotton swab | plain (fabric) | solid-color |
| cotton chintz | polished cotton fabric | plait(s) | braid(s) |
| | | poppers | snaps or grippers |
| cotton wool | cotton balls or absorbent cotton | press fasteners | grippers or snaps |
| | | PVA adhesive | white craft glue |
| crossways | crosswise | quick unpick | seam ripper |
| cushion pad | pillow form | ricrac | rickrack |
| DK wool | worsted yarn | selvedge | selvage |
| elasticated | elasticized | towelling | terrycloth |
| embroidery cotton | stranded floss | trousers | pants, slacks |
| filling (material) | stuffing | turn through | turn right side out |
| frill | ruffle | wadding | batting |
| haberdashery | notions | waistcoat | vest |
| knitting wool | yarn | widthways | widthwise |
| ladybird | ladybug | zip fastener | zipper |
| lengthways | lengthwise | | |